PUMP ON
THE PRAIRIE

PUMP
ON THE
PRAIRIE

A Chronicle of a Road Ranch

1859 — 1868

*   *   *

MUSETTA GILMAN

Best wishes to the Foulkes,

Musetta Gilman

10/23/84

HARLO   DETROIT

Printed in the United States by
Harlo Press / 50 Victor / Detroit Michigan 48203

DEDICATION

To Harold H. Gilman, Jeremiah's grandson, my husband,
who pioneered in Nebraska Soil Conservation; and to
Linda Lyon, my daughter, who teaches Nebraska
children

ACKNOWLEDGMENTS

A book does not become a reality without the help and encouragement of many people. I am particularly grateful to the research personnel of the National Archives, the historical libraries of Nebraska, Iowa, Wyoming, Oregon, and the western history department of the Denver Public library. I shall always be indebted to the late Raymond Dale, Mrs. Louise Small, and especially to Paul Riley, the research assistant of the Nebraska Historical library. I extend a special thank you to Mr. and Mrs. Lyle Bailey of Brady, Nebraska, and to Mrs. Amy Tuttle, and to my family.

A LETTER TO THE READER

Why another book about stage coaches, pony express and road ranches?

We are descendants of early Nebraska pioneer families. Consequently, I have had a "love affair" with Nebraska. While collecting pioneer human interest stories for Nebraska's school children, I was impressed with the fact that all the great movements in the development of the West came together in the Platte River Valley during the 1860's. Only little attention has been given to the men and women who provided for the needs of the thousands of travelers as they passed through the narrow corridor, particularly between Fort Kearny and Julesburg, Colorado on the Oregon Trail.

My husband's grandfather and great uncle were such providers. The Gilman road ranch near Fort McPherson, had a trading post and "hotel" accommodations. They traded with Sioux and Cheyenne. The ranch was a swing station for the Pony Express. It was a Ben Holladay Stage Station. The Gilmans furnished ties and wood for the Union Pacific Railroad. The ranch was Post Gilman Ranch during the Indian War of 1864-65. Jerry Gilman was one of the first County Commissioners of Lincoln County.

The Indians named John Gilman, We-Chox-Cha, the old man with the pump. The iron pump, a luxury item on the plains, supplied comfort to pilgrims, soldiers, adventurers, and V.I.P.'s involved in all these activities.

No attempt has been made to glamorize these people. The book is a simple chronicle pieced together from the newspapers of the day and from the written words of Gilmans' contemporaries.

TABLE OF CONTENTS

Chapter I

INTRODUCTION

It was Sunday morning, August 9, 1864; the place, a road ranch on the Oregon-California Trail some eighty miles west of Fort Kearny, Nebraska Territory.

John Kendall Gilman had fed and watered the teams belonging to Holladay's Overland Stage and put them back into the sod barn along with his own thoroughbred team and his beautiful roan riding horse. His other 17 head of horses and mules he left in the cedar corral beside the barn.

Although it was still early in the morning, the two hired men had taken the herd of trading oxen out into the valley to pasture on the seared blue stem and Indian grass that grew south of the heavily traveled wagon road.

A brassy morning sun beat down upon the parched Platte River Valley. The cedar buildings of the road ranch and the sod houses behind the trading post seemed blanketed in dust and heat. The flag on the crude staff before the store hung limp and motionless. John stopped and pumped himself a drink of cool water from the rusting pump that stood nearby.

The wide gates of the palisade stood open to the Trail welcoming any traveler who might be passing by. John glanced at the stage station looking forlorn and deserted off to the south of the large corral which had provided for so many pilgrims in the last three years. Two wagons stood in front of the station piled high with sacks of grain waiting to be unloaded.

When the morning chores were finished, John; his brother, Jerry and Herman Angell, who had so recently come to the ranch from Nebraska City, joined Martha, John's wife, and her sister in the sod house nearest the trading post. Martha's sister Jennie had just arrived the night before on the stage. Little George, John's two-year-old son, sat in his improvised high chair. Breakfast was ready.

As they sat at the table, John retold the news he had heard up at Cottonwood Springs the night before. The telegraph operator had rushed out to report that a wagon train had been set upon by a band of Cheyenne near Plum Creek Station the morning before. The wagons had been burned, the men massacred, and a woman and child were missing.

Martha's hands shook as she poured coffee from the big enameled pot. Sister Jennie repeated the details of her stage ride from Nebraska City. She shuddered as she remembered when the stage had stopped at Plum Creek to change teams, possibly only a few hours before this tragedy. She had shared the coach with several armed men, but they had seen no Indians. All the men had gone to sleep after they had left Midway.

Jennie had been so tired when she had arrived at the ranch, they had not told her of this frightening news. All were relieved that she had come through safely. What if the Indians had attacked the stage rather than a wagon train?

Everyone along the Trail from Julesburg to Fort Kearny knew that trouble was brewing among the Indians. The army had been uneasy, and had warned the ranchers to provide some means of protecting themselves. Daily patrols scouted the area around Fort Cottonwood some fifteen miles west of the Gilman ranch.

Jeremiah, attempting to reassure the women, commented that the Gilmans had never had Indian trouble. They had traded with both Cheyenne and Sioux, and had always treated them fairly. They had learned to speak the Indians' language. Hadn't Two Face, their trader, not more than a month ago, told them about a Cheyenne moving about trying to stir up trouble?

Herman Angell wondered if Gillette, his son and his partner who was helping Gillette build a new ranch down the Trail a few miles weren't taking chances. The men and their wives had been staying in one of Gilman's sod houses while they built their ranch. Herman remarked, "I heard them hitch up and leave before sun-up this morning. A man or two alone are a real temptation for any band of Indians on the warpath or not."

Suddenly the silence outside was shattered. Sounds of galloping horses, shouts and blood-curdling yells echoed around the ranch buildings. Out of the cloud of dust that seemed to rise from the river bottom to the north, they could see shiny, painted bodies and running horses. Around and around the buildings they rode. (Young bucks had done this before. After they had circled several times, they would come to a halt before the trading post to beg for tobacco or brown sugar.) Was this an attack or a prank?

John pushed the women back into the cabin and closed the door. The men hastily armed themselves. Martha moved little George to the bed in the corner away from the window and door.

The sounds no longer circled the ranch houses. There were still yelling, some shots and now the neighing of horses being driven from the corral. After about ten minutes which seemed like hours, John ventured out to see what was happening. Down the Trail to the southeast, he could see the Indians driving his mules and horses.

John watched helplessly, as the cloud of dust moved on down the valley. For the present those at the ranch were in no danger, but what of the Gillettes and his partner? Gilman ran to the barn, slipped a bridle on the big roan that could outrun any Indian pony and headed down the Trail.

Jeremiah and Herman, seeing the Indians had gone for the time being, and finding the two hired men had returned to the ranch were safe, hurried to harness the team from the sod barn and to hitch it to the buggy that stood nearby. They would take the women to the Fort where they would be safe.

Mrs. Gillette and a young woman with a baby in her arms came running to the Gilman house. Martha and Jennie tried to reassure the frightened women. No telling how long they might have to stay at the fort. The women gathered up clothing and food to be carried with them. Jennie, not knowing what else to do, placed the Gilmans' treasure box and Martha's silverware in the red checked tablecloth and tied the corners gypsy fashion.

Before the buggy was ready to go, they heard the roan's steady gallop and when the horse stopped, John slid down quickly. "The news is all bad," he said. "Hurry and hitch up one of the stage teams to the lumber wagon. All three were killed at the ranch. We must get their bodies before the bucks return."

Meanwhile, a caravan of coaches came in from the west. They halted and George H. Carlyle, an official of the Overland Mail, got out to inquire about their safety. The women told him of the tragedy that they would find down the road.

It must have been a couple of hours before they saw the wagon coming at full speed up the Trail. Martha had taken her good white sheets from her trunk to hide the gruesome sight from the weeping women.

The shocked women spurned the buggy and chose to ride in the wagon carrying their loved ones. A wagon seat was hastily attached to the wagon and Jennie climbed up beside the driver. She had managed to throw her unpacked carpet bag into the wagon, and holding the Gilman treasure bundle on her lap, she tried to comfort the frightened, broken-hearted women. The hired man cracked his whip and the wagon lunged forward toward the Trail.

Mat, little George, and the hastily packed clothing, the food, and a jug of water rode in the buggy with the other hired man. The spirited span of horses seemed to sense the urgency of their journey. John, still on the roan, cradling the Winchester under his arm, pulled out in front of the fort-bound procession. Over the roads as hard as pavement; over ruts that shook the wagon until the poor corpses rolled against their arrows; across dry creek beds, this desperate company made its way westward.

Mile after mile, the horseman, buggy, and wagon moved closer to safety. Nerves were taut. Any movement in the bluffs south of the trail or a glint of reflected sunlight from the sluggish river to the north, startled them. Martha was certain that she had seen a feathered head on a bluff overlooking Snell Canyon.

Jeremiah and Herman Angell stayed at the ranch. They would take a chance that the war party would go on down the trail and not return. Most Indian raids were unplanned and unpredictable.

As the Gilman party neared the fort, John could not help but think of his mother back in Bartlett, New Hampshire. He wondered if he would live to see her again. So much had happened to him and to Jeremiah since they left the rocky old New Hampshire farm.

What were these New Englanders doing so far from home? Why had they left their safe, peaceful New England home, where their ancestors had lived for almost two centuries, for this wild country which threatened them constantly with tornadoes, prairie fires, buffalo stampedes, rattlesnakes, blizzards, and now hostile Indians?

* * *

Young men all over the country were restless. They could not get jobs; money was tight and taxes high. Politics were disgusting. There was this problem with black-skinned people. War veterans, who had fought in the War with Mexico or those from the disasterous Mormon War found civilian life unbearable. Sober men whispered that another war was inevitable.

But in 1854, if a man could somehow make it west to the Missouri River, he could turn his back on all of that. Once he crossed the river, he had left the "States" and their problems. Congress had voted to open the vast territory, known before to Indians, fur traders, mountain men, and the trespassing emigrants going to Oregon or to California.

15

All kinds of people flooded the scattered settlements along the Missouri River in the late 1850's. Land-hungry farmers from Iowa, Missouri, and Illinois; duty-oriented soldiers; missionaries; European immigrants seeking homes or freedom; prostitutes; the runaways, and those who tagged along, came seeking their fortunes. Many were suffering from "gold fever." Educated New Englanders came. Some were the "black sheep" from aristocratic old families, others were dreamers or wanderers. Some came with wagons loaded with fine old furniture, others came without a penny in their pockets. But all seemed inoculated with the spirit of adventure.

Around the saloons, the livery stables, in front of the general stores, in hotel rooms, in these river settlements the story tellers passed on information to newcomers. Tobacco stained fingers drew maps in the dust. If there happened to be a newspaper published, copies were snatched before the ink was dry. Any traveler in from the West found himself the center of attention, bombarded by questions, and flattered into believing that he was an authority on the great new West.

It was not surprising then, that John Kendall Gilman and his younger brother, Jeremiah Chandler (known also as Jerry, Jed, or Jud) led their horses off of the Boulware ferry at Nebraska City Landing late in 1857. It had taken them three years to reach the west bank of the Missouri River.

The Gilman brothers left the old home in Bartlett, New Hampshire in 1854. Several friends from New Hampshire and Massachusetts had come to Iowa when the territory became a state in 1846. Among these friends was Sheldon Davis.

Davis had written about the many opportunities on the new frontier. When the Gilmans arrived in Iowa, they decided to build a mill and cracker on the Raccoon River in Greene County. They laid out a townsite and named it Kendricks. (Probably a Mr. Kendricks had invested in the venture.) But immigrants did not rush to settle this area, so the next year they moved to Warren County. Times were hard and money was tight so they disposed of the mill and turned their attention and their horses toward the Missouri River.

After the three years in the "wilds" of Iowa, the settlements around the river landing at Nebraska City seemed like cities to the New Englanders. For years the Missouri River had been a water highway for fur traders going north and west. The very location of this landing was advantageous. It was about 110 miles north of St. Joseph, Missouri, and 60 miles downstream from the Kanesville (Council Bluffs) and Omaha settlements.

The village referred to as Nebraska City sat upon the low bluffs out of the reach of the river that swirled and cut away banks in flood times. The approach from the waterfront (through the Kearny settlement) was so gradual that wagons had no great trouble transporting cargo from the river boats to the prairie.

Until 1854 the territory west of the Missouri River was considered Indian territory. However, there had been a steady stream of white men who had left the river from Missouri territory from Independence, Fort Leavenworth, and St. Joseph, moving into the valley of the Blue River, on into the Platte Valley and finally splitting off into California or into Oregon country since 1841. The great Mormon migration beginning in 1846 crossed the Missouri River near the Omaha settlements and marked a highway on the north side of the Platte. Treaty after treaty pulled land away from the Pawnee, Oto, and Omaha tribes. Finally the Kansas-Nebraska Act extended territorial organizations over all of the northern plains.

Before the territory was officially opened in 1854, white men were required to have a special permit from the Secretary of the Interior to settle in Indian territory. In the vicinity of Nebraska City, John B. Boulware, who had been operating a ferry at this point, built a log residence in 1852. Hiram Downs, Charles Cowles, and Charles Pierce also had permits.

During the middle 1840's the government constructed a fort near this landing. This was the first Fort Kearny (often spelled Kearney) but in 1848 the soldiers were removed and

17

a new Fort Kearny was built at the southernmost point of the big bend in the Platte, some 180 miles west of Nebraska City, to protect the immigrants going west.

As it always happened when Indian lands were opened to settlers, immigrants lost no time in spreading out into this new territory. In the three short years, not only Nebraska City had been laid out in lots, but Kearny, South Nebraska City, and Prairie City were surveyed and platted around this landing. Even an island in the Missouri River boasted of two towns—Woodlawn and Woodville.

Mollie Dorsey Sanford, a native of Indianapolis, came to Nebraska with her parents and seven brothers and sisters in 1857. She recorded in her diary of Thursday, April 10:

> Nebraska City, a nice name, but not much of a city. The town proper is situated on the hill or bluffs back from the river. But few houses are built yet. We are stopping where the town first settled, down near the river in Kearny City. This place is three years old. I hear there are churches and stores up in the other town. Here there are nothing but rude cabins and board shanties not even plastered. I see lots of men, but very few ladies and children. I heard one fellow shout, "Hurrah for the girls" as father marched his brood into the hotel parlor, and Mrs. Allen, our landlady, said,
> "I'm glad to see the girls." She is quite gossipy, and has already told us more than we can digest in a month. She says the place is full of gamblers, topers, and roughs of every description, and we will have to be very discreet. So I suppose we will hardly dare poke our noses outside the door for fear of contamination.

John and Jerry Gilman did not stop in Kearny City but made their way through the tangle of wagons, bull trains, horses, and teamsters to the village on the bluffs. The road leading from the Landing was called Main Street. Side streets were numbered. Here they saw a brickyard that appeared to have been operating for some time. The handsome brick building housing the Platte Valley Bank stood at the corner of 5th and Main. (S. F. Nuckolls, one of the founders of Nebraska City in 1854, had built this fine building with an eye to having a suitable territorial capitol should they be lucky in getting the territorial legislature to designate this new town as the capital. The capital remained in Omaha so Nuckolls used the building as a residence until 1856 when it became the bank.)

Other establishments were scattered along the dusty streets. There were general stores, a butcher shop, a blacksmith shop, and even a building housing a printing press. Nuckolls, Greever and Company had a lumberyard. The hotels had fancy names like the Planter House, the Nuckolls House or the Morton House. The Presbyterians had just completed a new church building, the finest in the territory. It even had a bell salvaged from a boat that had sunk in the Missouri River. The Methodist Episcopal congregation was boasting of a healthy growth. There were boarding houses and every store building with a second floor, rented rooms. Each establishment had its own barn, its own wood pile and its own privy out back.

This new town was populated chiefly by young men. Most of them were in their twenties, but many were still in their teens. John Gilman must have seemed old for he was twenty-nine. He was a big man with black hair and a full beard. His bulging muscles, stocky build, did not invite bullies to test his strength. Jerry was so different that people wondered if they were really brothers. John Nelson said that Jerry was as thin as a rail. His bright red hair which defied a comb, and his straggly red beard caused the Indians later to name him Po-te-sha-sha, meaning red whiskers. Although he was only twenty-three years old, he, too, was strong. Men about town soon accepted the New Hampshire boys. They were fond of jokes, could tell a good story, and brought a wealth of knowledge and experience to the new community.

Early in February 1858, word came up the river that the great freighting company of Russell, Majors, and Waddell having concluded another contract with the army, was considering Nebraska City as a shipping center for supplies being sent to the west over the Oregon Trail. The townspeople gathered around when Alexander Majors himself and Lieutenant DeBarry of the U.S. Army came to

19

town for a public meeting. Majors explained that the town would benefit in many ways if the freighting operation came up the river. The company anticipated that possibly 1000 wagons would start from this river port, some 1200-1500 men would be employed, and 8000 oxen and 800 mules would be assigned to this project. There were some conditions for the community to meet. The levee would need to be enlarged, facilities to handle at least five million pounds of freight at one time. A new highway must be built straight west of the city to connect with the well-traveled Platte Valley Road. Business houses were not to raise their prices, and high moral atmosphere must be maintained. Immediately, a committee of leading citizens met and formulated the resolutions outlining their willingness to meet the requirements, and these were submitted to the company.

On February 27, 1858, the official word came that Nebraska City had been selected as the depot for the great freighting firm. Supplies would be shipped up the river, loaded on freighting wagons and sent on their way to forts from the Missouri River to Salt Lake City. The boom was on.

Several projects were started immediately. First, the little villages around the landing were incorporated into the chosen city. Anyone who could use a hammer was employed to put up warehouses. A crew set out to build a bridge over Salt Creek. Kinney and Holly, local attorneys, became the authorized agents for the Freighting Company and men swarmed around their office seeking contracts for all kinds of services. J. Sterling Morton, who had eighty acres of land one mile west of town, laid out his farm in five acre lots.

How the ladies must have gossiped when the Majors family and four slaves moved into town in March. The newspaper reported that Majors had brought $40,000 in notes on a bank in Missouri.

As speculators and others seeking employment in the new river terminal poured in from everywhere, the need for local transportation became apparent. So the Gilmans opened up two livery stables, one at the old stand of George

Glines, and the other at the Kearney Hotel Stable. In the May 15th issue of the *Nebraska City News* the editor called attention to the new enterprise and commented upon the state of business in the new community. It read:

See the advertisement of Mr. Jack Gillman's livery establishments. He has two excellent livery stables and a fine lot of horses, buggies, etc. A year ago there was but one livery stable in the place and that one was obliged to close up on account of its not being a paying institution if we are not mistaken. Now there are three livery stables all doing a good business. Verily the town improveth if the times are hard.

(It might be appropriate to note here that there were other Gilmans in the area at this time. A John A. Gilman had come in 1854. He ran a butcher shop, an eating house, and farmed at various times. A William Gilman had a letter listed by the postmaster in the newspaper on August 14. As far as can be determined, none of these Gilman families were related.)

The activity on Main Street was described by Mollie Dorsey Sanford, the Indianapolis diarist mentioned before. She wrote in her diary on May 15, 1858:

Mrs. Burnham's rooms are in the second story of a large block. They are very pleasant, with low, deep windows where we can sit and view the street below. The lower story is used as headquarters for Majors, Russell & Company freighters. Today the streets are full of ox teams loading to start on a trip to Utah. All is commotion, the hallowing of the drivers, the clanking of chains and wagon masters giving orders. We noticed a splendid looking fellow who rides a mouse-colored mule, and who grew more important as he became conscious of our notice. We said, 'Now that fellow is too nice looking for that business. He is certainly a professional gentleman, perhaps acting as foreman for pastime. It could not be his occupation.' While admiring him today from our porch, I was somewhat disenchanted to hear him roar out to one of the men,

21

'Put them thar pans down thar, you gallipin fool, an con hur.'

Then someone came up and accosted him with, 'Hello! Pete!'and when Pete raised his eyes to gaze at us, somehow the glory faded, and we found that he was only plain Peter Byram from Pike County, Missouri. Alas! for romance, Peter.

Livery stables in river ports were wise investments. For such institutions in 1858 brought all kinds of people to do business. For a modest fee one could "park" his horse there and be certain that it would be carefully fed and watered. A "rent-a-horse" service made it possible for land speculators to transport likely customers out to look at available land. A fine horse and buggy could impress a young lady if her mother allowed her to go for a buggy ride on a Sunday afternoon. A stable boy on a horse could substitute for courier service. This was especially important since there were no telegraph lines nor telephones. The livery stable was a natural place for men to congregate. They swapped horses, gossip, opinions, and deals over a watering trough or a curry comb.

And there was plenty of gossip—with all the building going on; the arrival of supplies and all kinds of freight as soon as the ice broke up in the river. And people and more people scampered onto shore as the river boats anchored along the shore.

But the most exciting news came in September. Stories found their way into the conversations concerning a new discovery of gold in Colorado (then Kansas Territory.) The *Kansas City Journal* featured a long article about the mountaineers that came back with old John Cantrell of Westport. Ten had come in for supplies and showed specimen of gold found in the Pike's Peak area. By the first of October trains were loading for the mines even in the Nebraska river towns. If you had not contracted the "gold fever" when gold was discovered in California a decade ago, you were certainly exposed now. Every issue of the newspapers along the frontier carried news from the Pike's Peak—Cherry Creek region.

John Gilman caught the "germ" in October. Business brought up the river by boats had already slowed down. As soon as the ice began to appear in the river, the boats and barges tied up in their home ports. There was already much unemployment in the river settlements.

Isaac Sager (also a mature 29-year-old), and Jerome Dauchy, a 24-year-old carpenter, made a deal with John. Each would take two horses and a mule. They would make the trip to the mines, planning to be gone for two months. They did not intend to mine or even prospect for gold. They hoped to set up an express delivery service between the mines and the banks in Nebraska City.

Chapter II

THERE'S A LONG, LONG TRAIL . . .

John Gilman, Jerome Dauchy, and Isaac Sager, the three would-be expressmen, prepared as best as they could for the long trip ahead. The mules were loaded with camping equipment, food, medicine, bedding and extra clothing. Since the animals could not live "off of the land" so late in the season, even some grain went into the packs.

Traveling in October had its advantages, however. Summertime travelers reported hot, dry winds loaded with alkali dust that burned faces and cracked lips. Summer also brought sudden thunderstorms. It was frightening to both animals and pilgrims when lightning played across the sky, clouds boiled up into grotesque banks. Hail frequently accompanied these sudden storms. These pebbles of ice could stampede a herd of cattle or buffalo. Its fury tore wagon tops or tents to shreds.

There was less chance of meeting the terror of the plains, called a "cyclone," in October. Tornadoes in late spring or early summer would descend without warning from tumor-like clouds. Clouds that shaped into a funnel, in seconds elongated into a wasp's nest, changing again into a black rope. Swinging from side to side, it pulverized wagons, scattered stock and drove straw into oak wagon tongues.

The first frost had been on October the sixth, so the plague of insects had lost some of its torture. Mosquitoes, flies, ticks, and bed bugs tormented the summer travelers and followed them into the ranch houses and soddies.

As the trio prepared to leave Nebraska City they were told that a man named Smedley said that this gold business was a humbug. Others returning urged people not to start out until spring. But groups of people were moving through the river towns every day. The *Nebraska City News* counted fifty-two in one day. (Wagons continued to be loaded and sent out as late as November.)

On the departure day, a light mist hung over the river, and the air was clear and cold. A last tightening of the ropes that bound the supplies, a check of the saddle cinches, and the three men mounted their horses and headed out. Main Street was deserted at this early hour.

West and northwest leaving the bluffs near the river, they crossed the now dry bed of North Table Creek, past the camps of the freighters. Some of the freighters were preparing to move out. Others had already stretched out along the well-traveled trail.

At night they pitched their tent, and cooked their meal at camp grounds where others had stopped. There were still pilgrims in their canvas covered wagons on the road.

Mile after mile the well-shod Gilman horses moved along the road that meandered through small settlements and well improved farms. In 1858 travelers were using what was known as the "ox-bow" route from Nebraska City. This north and west trail took them through a settled area for about fifty miles. (Today it would be near Otoe, west then north on the ridge between Weeping Water, Wabash, and Elmwood. They would pass southwest of the outskirts of Murdock, then Ashland, over the rolling hills past Swedeburg. The trail wound over the hills in Butler County passing north of David City. They entered the wide Platte Valley just south of Bellwood.)

There were good camping places on the Platte bottoms. The traveling was easier now as the horses and riders followed the well-traveled sandy road of the valley. The river lay about two miles from the trail.

When they reached the camp referred to as Round

Pond, they knew that they were near the famous old Leavenworth road (north and west of Kenesaw). Fifteen more miles and they would stop at Fort Kearny.

The flag was flying over the little cluster of buildings marking this first knot of civilization since they had left the settlements near Nebraska City. It scarcely deserved the name of "fort" since it was just a group of barracks, officers' quarters, stables, and warehouses planted on the south bank of the Platte River. Chilling rains had been falling, and they had had to break the ice tissue on the small water holes so that the horses could drink.

The three horsemen stopped at the fort and visited with the soldiers while the horses rested. About a mile farther west one branch of the road that brought travelers across the Platte River from Omaha joined the Trail. They passed a sod hut which might have been used for a stage station but no one seemed to be around. About two miles west of the Fort, was another sod house, and another branch road from the Omaha road. A crude sign labeled it, "Central City store." They stopped, and visited with a man who called himself Jack Morrow. He told them that a company from St. Joseph had come out with the intentions of establishing a town here on the edge of the military reservation. Mr. Pfouts, Alex Constant, and a Col. Scott laid out the town site. Jack had bought the store when these men decided to go back to civilization to spend the winter. The Nebraska City travelers made camp here and visited with others who were headed west.

Heading out as early as it was light, the three passed the next good camping ground which was some 17 miles west of the Fort and traveled on up the Trail to the next stopping place near the mouth of Plum Creek. Here was plenty of wood and water.

The river valley corridor was sharply defined now. The loess hills to the south which had first appeared like giant, round beads strung along the valley, gradually grew higher and higher. The Trail was almost a straight line about two miles from the river. Along this stretch of road, the few pilgrims that were making their way west, were gathering buffalo chips to burn as fuel. The men spent the night at a campground a few rods south of the Trail. They not only shared a buffalo chip campfire but good conversation with those from a wagon train who hoped to get to Denver before the weather closed in.

Having been told by early explorers that this region was a desert area, the travelers were pleasantly surprised at the beauty of the valley. The prairie grass was now bronze and olive green. Occasionally a clump of sumac glowed red against the willows on the islands in the river. Flocks of wild geese darkened the evening sky. Antelope darted across the road in front of the horses.

They found only peace and quiet in the valley. They saw no buffalo herds three or four miles wide, nor bands of roving Indians who might slip into camp at night and make off with the horses. Yet travelers who had gone this way before, told stories of wild stampedes, and the loss of precious horses. Conversations around the campfires were always about the same. The men talked of gold mines, of fertile land for farming, the new dimension of commerce that Russell, Majors, and Waddell were bringing to the west. The women talked of homes that they had left, of sickness, of the accidents and other disasters that threatened anyone who ventured into this unknown land.

Day after day the men followed the well-worn road westward. In many places the trail was a mesh of interlacing ruts on this south side of the river. A few small spring-fed streams found their way to Mother Platte. Occasionally they could see travelers on the north side of the river—going to Salt Lake City, no doubt. When the long hours in the saddles became unbearable, the men walked and led the horses.

At last they arrived at the well-publicized camping grounds known as Cottonwood Springs. Immigrants on their way to California or Oregon had rested here, did their washing and baked their bread before they traveled on. The camp with its good spring water and abundance of good wood nearby, had been a haven for travelers for many years.

27

Earlier in the fall, Isador P. Boyer (who limped about on a wooden leg) and the well-known fur trader, Robideau, had built a crude building on the north side of the Trail near the campground. They imported some canned goods, some ammunition, and a barrel of whiskey and were in business.

When the Gilman party stopped to rest, to reshoe their horses, they met Richard Darling, a young man from Omaha. He had just come in with a load of timber wolf pelts. He seemed glad to visit with the travelers from Nebraska City. He showed them the highly-prized skins of these giant wolves. The hair was long and silky. Some were almost black and others were nearly white. They sold for $2.50 each. He had used the simple method of poisoning. The poison saved ammunition and the pelts came off unblemished. Large numbers of these wolves would follow wagon trains and eat crumbs, bones, and broken-down oxen.

Darling pointed out a site on the south side of the Trail across from Boyers where he planned to build a storehouse as soon as the weather cleared in the spring. He had great hopes that many would build stations along the Trail. He told how during the Mormon War in 1857, he had been employed by the government as a dispatch carrier. He rode from Fort Bridger on the California Trail to Fort Leavenworth in four days, during which time he never slept. He ate his food as best he could while riding at full speed. He only stopped long enough to change horses at the stage relay stations which were few and far between.

Others at Boyer's store warned the men that wood would be scarce for the next 200 miles. So Sager filled the empty grain sacks with wood and added them to the other supplies.

Through a stretch of flat country, through sandy braids of ruts, over sandy ridges and by the third day they reached another landmark—O'Fallons Bluff. In this vicinity Moore and Grimes had a store and acted both as representatives of the government and agents for Majors and Waddell. (In 1856 they had driven 500 head of cattle for Majors, headed for Laramie. A blizzard caught them and all the animals died and these men barely escaped.)

Some forty weary miles farther they arrived at the Laramie Crossing. Here the California-bound travelers crossed the South Platte River and headed northwest. But those going to Denver followed the right bank of the South Platte. The trail was so faint that Dauchy was certain that it was no trail at all. Although there were evidences that men and horses had been along, there appeared to have been only three or four wagons.

The next seventy-four miles were torture. The nights were colder, they could notice the higher altitude so the horses rested more frequently. Here was Beaver Creek. The banks were steep and although the icy water was only about three feet deep, the stream at this point was about twenty feet wide.

Fortunately they caught up with another group of horsemen also headed toward the famous peak with its promise of yellow gold. These men shared their field glasses and all could see the faint images of both Long's and Pike's Peaks. A band of Cheyenne Indians were camped near the trail. They seemed friendly enough. Each rider, however, checked his side arms for all the Indians seemed to be well armed with bows and arrows. (Cheyenne were known to try to stampede animals by lying flat in the grass, then rising up with a whoop.)

Their path wound through this arid land which produced only cactus and soap weed. After crossing a dry channel, they camped in a cottonwood grove. They gathered dry wood and for the first time since they left O'Fallons Bluff, they were warm.

Over a sandy bluff, across the wild ravine, the faithful horses carried them to Fort St. Vrain. This unique fort, built by traders, never occupied by troops, had been a landmark for many years. The roof now had fallen in, but the sturdy cement, gravel, and deer hair walls still stood. This crude establishment was located where the South Platte River turned abruptly from a northern to an eastern course.

One of the men in the other party reckoned that it was best to leave the river here and travel some forty-five miles southeast to Cherry Creek. (Those traveling this way later would not come this far west before heading for Cherry Creek.)

Chapter III

1859
"GO WEST, YOUNG MAN"

Gilman, Dauchy, and Sager arrived at the settlements along Cherry Creek about the first of November 1858. Already the rugged mountain peaks to the west and the southwest were snow-covered. Frequent snow showers pelted the three hundred or so people who were frantically building shelters on both sides of this little stream. Almost all of the miners and tradespeople were still living in tents.

All up and down the river banks men were searching for that elusive yellow dust called gold. Tempers were short and arguments blossomed everywhere.

It was impossible to determine how much truth there was in the amount of gold being found. The tales in the tent saloon were large enough but there seemed to be no miner rich enough to send gold dust back to the banks in Nebraska City. Those who appeared to be prosperous saw the long, hard winter before them. Supplies, even fuel, were being sold or bartered at exorbitant prices.

After a few days of rest for men and horses, the three would-be couriers headed back up the trail toward home. The weather was clear and cold but the sun shone every day. After they had rested for a few days at Moore and Grimes ranch near O'Fallon's Bluff, they found traveling easier. Even this well-traveled trail was practically deserted. Only a

Main Street, Nebraska City, from a sketch by Alfred E. Matthews

few wagons that had loaded and moved out in November appeared on the road.

Before they were safety back in Nebraska City, John Gilman and Jerome Dauchy decided that as soon as the weather was settled in the spring, they were somehow going to acquire a bull train and come again to the mines. But Isaac Sager could only thnk of his tired body, the long weary miles on horseback. What would it be like walking beside a yoke of slow-moving bulls? (Isaac Sager was not listed on the territorial census of 1860, but he returned to Nebraska City in June 1861 and enlisted in Company F., First Nebraska Regiment, mustered in as a private on July 3, 1861. In 1864, he came back to Nebraska City on sick leave and died July 5, 1864.)

The cold weather during January and February of 1859 had not slowed the activity around the little river port. It seemed that everyone who had a wagon or money to buy one was planning to go to the mines in the spring. Businessmen were ordering supplies from St. Louis to be delivered as soon as the boats could bring them up the river. The agents for Russell and Majors were already drawing up sub-contracts for the hauling of supplies to both the army posts and to the mines.

When Hawke and Nuckolls, the most prominent merchants in Nebraska City, announced that they were sending merchandise to Colorado City very early in the spring, Gilman offered to haul part of the cargo.

Jerry Gilman was reluctant to give up the good business at the livery stables, so John hired Henry Clifford, a strong, adventure-loving young man, to pilot the second wagon. The Clifford family had come to Nebraska City in 1855. The father had operated a hotel for a time. Later he made yoke for oxen. Henry had done all kinds of work. He was especially handy with hammer and saw.

Although there had been one or two bad storms during the winter, the roads remained open and the spring came early. Generally, the wagons did not start west until April or May when the oxen could survive on the grass along the Trail. But many were eager to head out as soon as possible, so some started in March. They included grain in their cargo.

John Gilman and Henry Clifford were among the early ones. The going was slow, but they were unusually lucky in losing neither stock nor merchandise. They delivered the goods to the agent in the shanty town. They rested at Cherry Creek before they started the long trek home. Cherry Creek was not the same tent city that Gilman had seen in November. The population had doubled. Many miners had continued to come by the way of Santa Fe. Crude buildings had been completed; and a store that had operated in a tent last winter was now comfortable in a double cabin.

Promoters had been busy during the winter. Guide books and other forms of propaganda had flooded the East. But many who had spent the cold winter in Colorado looking for gold, were disillusioned. Empty freight wagons returning to civilization were soon being hired for human transportation. When John and Henry reached O'Fallons Bluff, pilgrims were already turning back. Much bitterness was directed to those who had promoted the stampede to the Rocky Mountains.

Many changes were taking place along the Trail. Bob Williams and Thomas Conroy were building a ranch at the foot of O'Fallons Bluff. Russell had sent crews out to repair or to rebuild new stage stations for the Salt Lake Stage Line. The Western Stage Company was planning to send stages from Omaha to Denver and a fleet to move from one digging to another. When the Gilman wagons stopped at Box Elder Canyon two or three miles west of Cottonwood Springs, they were surprised to find Gilman's old friend, Sheldon Davis, erecting a supply depot for the stage company. It was about a mile or so west of the stage station.

When they stopped at Cottonwood Springs, they admired Dick Darling's project that he described to them last winter. About every fifteen miles or so, men were building sod shanties. These were especially appearing around old camp grounds.

By the time that Gilman and Clifford finally got back to Nebraska City, a new wave of gold fever had reached the

34

river. This was the result of newspaper articles that were appearing throughout the country.

Because there was so much interest in this new gold strike in Colorado, several important newspapers had sent reporters to the mines in early 1859. Among these reporters were such famous journalists as Horace Greeley, Henry Villard, and Albert Richardson. Greeley had arrived just in time to report the Clear Creek discovery northwest of the Cherry Creek diggings. John Gregory, a Georgia "Cracker," had struck a bonanza, and the news leaked out in May, 1859.

It was sometime in June that the Gilman wagons rested back in Nebraska City. Never had there been so much traffic coming up the river. Each boat disgorged supplies and people into the already overcrowded towns. There was still time this season to take more wagons to the diggings.

John set out to find a buyer for the livery stables, and Jerry attempted to collect the outstanding bills. (He even sued a man for $25 unpaid feed bill.) Henry Clifford got out his trusty tools and repaired the wagons. Jerome Dauchy came by and offered to help outfit the wagon train.

This time the brothers purchased their own merchandise to sell. They kept two good riding horses for scouting or possibly for the return trip from Denver. Wagons and oxen brought a good price anywhere in the West.

Besides the regular trade items of food, clothing, ammunition, and whiskey, they loaded one wagon with iron pipes, wheelbarrows, tools, and a luxury item—a fine red, iron pump. The pump was a sign of affluence on the frontier where a windlass and bucket were the usual means of getting water from the well.

Day after day, the four men gee-ed and haw-ed their clumsy oxen through the settled area near Nebraska City. The valley of the Platte looked even longer than it had the first time they had gone to Denver. Dauchy was impressed at the number of houses that had sprung up along the way since they had come this way last October.

Where the road from St. Joseph and Leavenworth joined

with the Nebraska City road, there was a stable, a dwelling, and a store. It had been named Valley City. The store appeared to be doing a lively business. (Later, pilgrims would refer to this new settlement as Dogtown, possibly because there was a large prairie dog city in the vicinity according to Frank Young, who traveled through the area in 1865.)

It was getting late in the afternoon as they approached Fort Kearny. The trail was becoming more and more congested. Some trains had halted to visit the post office at the fort, or to make a purchase from the sutler's store. No one was allowed to camp on the military reservation so the majority of those in the vicinity were making their way to the camping grounds around another cluster of sod houses called Kearny City.

Jack Morrow was still in his sod store but a new town had sprung up in the area. When the daily stage and mail route was laid out, John Young, J. E. Boyd, a Col. Rankin, a Dr. Henry, and Lorin Miller, all from Omaha, formed the new town, called Kearny City. Central City disappeared. The business shacks were all made of sod, and before the summer was over, the town became "Dobytown" to the freighters and traders along the trail.

More travelers were crossing the Platte River from the north, coming from Omaha and Council Bluffs. While the Gilman wagons were making their way through the dust, a stage coach dashed by. The station lay between the fort and Kearny City.

The heat, the dust, and the flies were almost unbearable. The oxen were unhitched from the wagons, driven to the river, where they waded into the cooling water. Grazing spots were scarce since so many trains had stopped here.

Only minor problems had plagued the four "bull whackers" as they made their way westward the next day. But after they had left the camp at the seventeen mile point, the deep ruts and sand began to tell on the heavily loaded wagons.

Later freight wagons would be especially built for

36

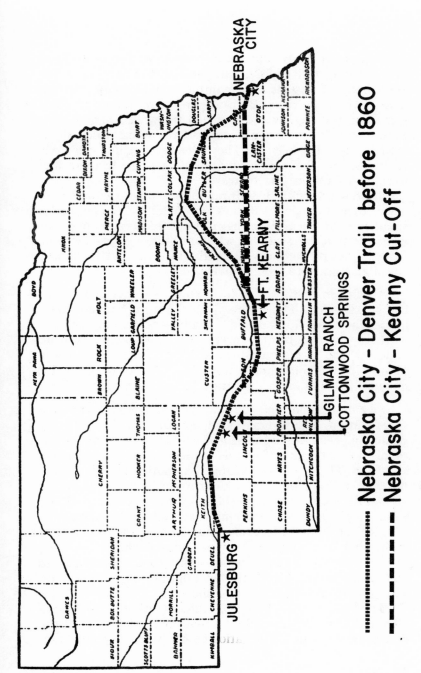

———— Nebraska City - Denver Trail before 1860

– – – – Nebraska City - Kearny Cut-Off

Trail showing location of the Gilman ranch

carrying such loads, but these wagons had already been over the long trail before. The men pulled away from the main body of wagons, and gambled on the sandy bottom land next to the river. Both wagons were unloaded. They jacked up the wagons and removed the wheels. The wheels were soaked in the river to expand the wood which fitted within the iron rim. They loaded again carefully redistributing the heavy equipment, and made their way back to the main line of travel.

Slowly and painfully they made their way to Plum Creek where there was a mail station and William Lee operated a small store in his soddie. They did not find repairs here but were told that Pat Mullally, who was building a ranch some fifteen miles further on west, might have some extra wheels. But Pat could offer only advice.

About ten or fifteen miles farther, another ranch was being expanded. The rancher, Dan Smith, had not been home when the Gilman and Clifford wagons had stopped on their way back from Denver a few weeks before. Now he had sold one of his buildings to W. S. Peniston who was planning a log house and a store. (A. J. Miller would be his partner. It is not known if Miller had arrived at this time.)

Five more miles and the stage company was repairing a stage station. The foreman said that this was the half way station between Atchison, Kansas and Denver. More wagon repair, more doping of wheels, and the two wagons moved slowly on. The valley was relatively smooth and wide for the next ten miles. They moved away from the rutted trail and guided the wagons through the tall grass. Fortunately there were a very few little streams that had to be crossed.

As they neared the campground called the fifteen mile point, they crossed a small ravine. Not the wheels this time, but an axle broke. There was nothing to do but to unload and set up camp. With luck they might be able to trade for a wagon from pilgrims along the trail.

The four travelers had paid little attention to the Indian village that huddled beside the road after they had left the stage station. Soon a delegation came to beg, and ended up by trading some unusually fine buffalo robes for some of the supplies intended for miners along Cherry Creek.

While the men were trying to repair the wagon, and to make a comfortable camp, many wagon trains halted. Some to camp overnight, others to visit, and still others to trade two footsore oxen for one good trail oxen.

Although the flat valley floor was about three to five miles wide between the rugged loess hills and the river, here was an ideal camp site. The small ravine was spring fed, and the road followed a silty bench between the hills and the sandy flood plain near the river. The river was about a half mile from the road. Far across the valley were deep canyons lined with thick growths of red cedar trees, so thick that the trees had grown tall and straight.

Several days passed. Pilgrims and Indians persisted in trading. A load of wood brought across the valley for their own use as fuel, was sold in a day. The footsore oxen gorged themselves on the rich "bottoms" grass and once more became trade merchandise. The men made a decision.

It would be late summer before they could hope to get to Denver this season. Others on the trail were having difficulties getting supplies, water, and fuel. Why not build a road ranch here at this natural camping ground? The one wagon was good enough to travel back to Nebraska City for more supplies. When winter came, they could trap, trade with the Indians, or make it back to civilization.

The water table was high in the valley, so it was no problem to dig a well. Into the well lined with strong cedar posts from the canyons to the south, they put in the fine red pump. The Indians christened John Gilman, We-Chox-Cha, the old man with a pump. Pilgrims stopped to admire and to enjoy the cold, clear water from the tin cup suspended from the pump.

Using the new plow, meant for the vegetable growers of Denver, and the wheelbarrows, intended to cradle ore, the four men cut strips of rich sod into bricks and soon two sod houses established a service station for travelers, just fifteen to seventeen miles east of the famous Cottonwood Springs.

1859 and 1860 marked the beginning of a series of

Iron Pump on the Prairie still used at old Fort Laramie

trading posts called road ranches (the singular often spelled ranche) between Fort Kearny and the separation of the trail leading north to Fort Laramie, or south to Denver and the new gold mines of Colorado. For the next decade these unique enterprises supported the communication and transportation that crossed the continent. The ranchers, mostly young men, were as varied in character as could be.

Description of road ranches varied, first, depending upon the time when the traveler visited the ranch, and the type of people operating the establishment. Sir Richard Burton, an English world traveler, described several in his bood *The Look of the West 1860 Across the Plains to California.*

Near Troy, Kansas Territory—"Squalor and misery were imprinted upon the wretched log-hut, which ignored the duster and broom, and myriad of flies disputed with us a dinner consisting of doughnuts, green and poisonous with saleratus, suspicious eggs in a massive greasy fritter, and rusty bacon, intolerably fat."

At a place between Ashpoint and Guittards he stated: "The house and kitchen were clean, the fences neat; the ham and eggs, the hot rolls and coffee, were fresh and good, and although drought had killed the salad we had abundance of peaches and cream, an offering of French to American taste . . . "

Before they reached Little Sandy he wrote: "The ranch was a nice place for invalids, especially for those of the softer sex. Upon the floor of the foul 'Doggery' lay, in seeming promiscuous heap, men, women, children, lambs, and puppies, all fast in the arms of Morpheus, many under the influence of a much jollier god."

Burton did not always distinguish between the stage station facilities and the so-called road ranch, so his description of the Lodge-Pole Station might well have described a ranch in the vicinity:

"The hovel fronting the creek was built like an Irish shanty or a Beloch hut, against a hillside, to save one wall, and it presented a fresh phase of squalor and wretchedness. The mud walls were partially papered with 'Harper's Magazine,' 'Frank Leslie' and the New York Illustrated News;' the ceiling was a fine festoon-work of soot, and the floor was much like the ground outside, only not nearly so clean. In a corner stood the usual bunk, a mass of mingled rags and buffalo robes; the center of the room was occupied by a rickety table, and boxes, turned-up on their long sides, acted as chairs. The unescapable stove was there, filling the interior with the aroma of meat. As usual, the materials for ablution, a 'dipper' or cup, a dingy tin skillet of scanty size, a bit of coarse, gritty soap, and a public towel, like a rag of gunny sac, were deposited upon a rickety settle outside."

Dr. C. M. Clark, who also traveled in 1860, commented in his book *A Trip to Pike's Peak and Notes Along the Way:*

Smith's ranch is a small building constructed of logs, where liquor, preserved fruits, etc. are to be had. Why these buildings, or stations, are called ranches, is more than I can say. The proprietors do not cultivate the soil, nor do they raise stock, they merely squatted along this line of travel, for the purpose best known to themselves. These miscalled ranches throughout the Platte Valley are essentially, one and the same thing; sometimes differing in size and style of construction—some are of the adobe species, while others are constructed of rough logs and poles, and sometimes we meet with one built of squared cedar posts that look very neat. The proprietors are generally rude specimens of humanity, in every sense of the word, and many of them dress in garments made from elk and deer skins, ornamented with long fringes of the same materials up and down the seams; their hair and beard, in many cases, had been suffered to grow, giving them a ferocious look and in fact, they are as primitive as the country they inhabit. In order to insure the respect and confidence of the Indians, many of them have squaw wives, who inhabit a lodge nearby.

(This was a reference to the Daniel L. Smith ranch some ten miles east of the Gilman ranch.)

Lower 96 ranch building taken about 1896, showing cedar construction of buildings and corral. This is probably Smith's west ranch mentioned by Dr. C. M. Clark 1860[a].

Another Englishman making his way along the Oregon Trail in 1863 described a typical ranch.

It must not be supposed that these ranches imply farming on any scale whatever; they are simply business stations to meet the wants of the emigrants and travelers westward, and therefore each mainly consists of one room, which serves for store, grog-shop, and bedroom by night. In the smaller ones, and they are by far the most numerous, the stock in hand may be set down as consisting of much pork, ham and a few pounds of coffee, salt, pepper, vinegar, pear ash, soda, flour, butter, eggs, corn, dried apples, peaches in tins, and oysters also, with a Falstaffian proportion of a vile compound of whiskey and I know not what, which is popularly known as 'bust head' or 'forty rod' because the unfortunate imbiber is seriously effected in either brain or legs, or even both, before he had gone the distance . . . But one of their great sources of wealth lay in 'trading' oxen. For this purpose they begin with a few of their own, and when a man passes with a foot-sore ox which can go no further, they sell the traveler a fresh one at their own rate, while a dollar or two is considered the rule of the road for the faded ox; . . . it will not be surprising that these ranchers make a pile quickly."

Frank Helvey, an old freighter, described one such building which he said was fairly typical of all stage stations and ranches along the trail:

The building was made of hewn logs and was about 36' by 16' and 8' high. The roof was supported by a long ridgepole. It might have a small attic reached by a ladder. The floor was punceon, and slabs of hardwood were dressed and matched together over log sills. There was a large fireplace at one end, built of rock with a chimney outside. The doors were broad boards cleated together, hung on wooden or leather hinges. The windows were one or two sashes containing eight panes of glass. Lime and plaster chinked the cracks between the logs and the walls were whitewashed each year. Ill-matched boards covering joists were pegged, and guns, meat, and other articles were hung from the pegs.

44

Many such buildings were partitioned by rough board walls, or muslin curtains hung on wires. The furniture was homemade. The beds, if there were beds, were built of native timber fitted with board slats or laced with heavy cords to support the 'straw ticks' or feather beds. The doorsteps were broad logs hewn flat on top. It was common to see elk horns hung over the door.

Mrs. Carrington, the wife of Col. Henry Carrington, on the Trail in 1865-66 gave a detailed description of a typical post. By this time many women had been at the ranches. (Some had gone back to the States after the trouble with the Indians.) She said that many of the stations had three rooms. Room #1, about 10' by 12', had a plank counter with shelves behind. On these shelves were the trading merchandise and the liquor. All kinds of merchandise from spices, tobacco, canned fruit, whips to ready-made clothing, were for sale. (From the cash books kept at the McDonald ranch, it would appear that by 1865 the important ranches were as well equipped as a country store in the States.)

In room #2, according to Mrs. Carrington, one might find the eating quarters. There would be an iron stove for cooking, a pine table and benches or perhaps crude chairs. The huge coffee pot stayed on the stove at all times. The fare varied from one ranch to another according to the skill of the cook. In this room travelers and helpers exchanged news and views. Profanity was common, and arguments enlivened the conversation.

In room #3 was space for sleeping. Most travelers spread their blankets or buffalo robes on the floor, since more people could be accommodated in this manner. Men, women, and children often shared the same room. Mrs. Carrington said that the ladies in her party slept outside in tents rather than share such a room.

The Gilman ranch started with two sod houses (Census 1860) and a corral. As the business grew, so grew the ranch buildings. By 1863, the main building had at least two rooms. (Eugene Ware) John Y. Nelson, who worked for the Gilmans off and on all the time they were on the Trail, said:

"They had started one of the largest ranches along the road, and when I arrived they were at work building the shanty, helped by six men, who were lumbering up the logs.

"I made a trial engagement with them for one month. My duties were the same as at Billy Hill's, and my pay fifteen dollars per month. This was small but I knew it would soon increase.

"We had stabling for one hundred and seventy-five horses, and a large corral capable of holding any number of emigrants."

After the demise of the pony express, the Gilman ranch became a swing station for Holladay's stage lines so a stage station was added to the cluster of buildings. When the trouble with Indians became serious, the ranch was fortified.

When Frank C. Young traveled to Denver in 1865, he wrote:

Gilman's used to be a favorite trading post with the Sioux, but quite recently has been the scene of some lively scraps with some former savage patrons. It is now a military station of some importance, the soldiers' quarters occupying about a dozen log houses."

John Y. Nelson, describing a scene at the ranch in 1866:

"I took possession of the fort, which was about forty steps away from the ranche, and consisted of a circular room some twelve feet in diameter, excavated in the ground, with an underground passage from it running to the stables. A stockade surrounded it, absolutely impregnable, at least from attacks by Indians."

So it was that these unique institutions, combinations of trading posts, hotels, blacksmith shops, livery stables, city halls were anchor posts for a line of civilization which tied California and other western settlements to the Union. Nebraska was still a territory in 1859, so there was no law nor taxes out on the sea of grass. It was a man's world, for few women came for a year or two because life by necessity was primitive. Some ranchers stayed on after the traffic on

46

McDonald's road ranch, Cottonwood Springs, Lincoln County, Nebraska Territory

the trail halted for the winter. They serviced the stage line, or trapped, or traded with the Indians. Other ranchers drifted back to civilization to come again in the spring. This was government land (or Indian land) so one did not register a title to his ranch site. He "squatted" and later on, if the land were surveyed and he wished to have title, he could file a claim. In almost every instant, the rancher moved across the river after the railroad came in 1866, or he left the country to seek his living elsewhere and for a time this thread along the trail reverted back to buffalo, grass, and prairie fires.

Chapter IV

1860
SOBERING SIXTIES

The new year, 1860, came in cloudy and cold. By this time the Gilmans had established a routine at the ranch. A typical day began as soon as it was light enough to see. The cattle were herded out to feast on the dry prairie grass or fed the hay the men had managed to put up in a stack near the corral. Jerome Dauchy did the cooking and kept an eye out for the chance traveler who might happen by. Every day when the weather permitted, the men hitched the oxen to the one good wagon and drove across the valley to the broad canyon so full of good red cedars.

The cedars were cut, trimmed and hauled across the flat river valley to the ranch site. The "trimmings" were sawed into length for firewood. It was a constant struggle to keep themselves warm and to get a woodpile high enough to sell to the immigrants who were certain to come down the trail early in the spring.

Stages continued to pass at irregular intervals. The men were cheered by the sight of the dashing horses and coach. It meant that they were not entirely cut off from civilization. Once a week, one of them would ride up the trail to Cottonwood Springs to get the mail. The newspapers might be two or three weeks old, but every issue and item was carefully read and reread.

This was the year for the presidential election. This

campaign was most complicated because of serious national problems. It was evident early in the year that there was a serious split in the Democratic Party over slavery, especially in the territories. Ranchers along the trail were interested in the faction in the Republican Party who were supporting a homestead law. (One of the campaign slogans was, "Vote Republican, and vote yourself a farm!") More and more Southerners were stating publicly that they had the right to secede from the Union if the elections did not go as they chose.

But the news that most interested the ranchers was the activities of the great enterprises of the Russell, Majors, and Waddell Company. If the company did send all these freighting trains and a regular stage line, every rancher had opportunities to profit from storage, from the sale of hay, and to market surplus trail oxen.

But the newspapers did not report what was going on behind the closed doors of the business office of this Russell, Majors, and Waddell transportation empire of the West. When these three ambitious freighters and businessmen had pooled their resources in 1854 to win the monopoly of transportation contracts with the federal government for transporting goods to remote outposts in the West, each man contributed something unique besides his capital investment. Waddell was a shrewd merchant, Alexander Majors was a freighter who knew more about freighting than anyone in the country. (Some say that he invested the most money.) But it was William Russell who brought imagination and a gambling man's techniques.

The company quickly gained a reputation for dependability and integrity. The first two years, they fulfilled all their commitments to supply the army posts on the Santa Fe Trail, and along the California-Oregon Trail, showed a profit for the company, and increased both the personal fortunes and the reputations of the partners.

In 1857, the company staggered from the tremendous loss when they tried to supply the unfortunate "Mormon War" troops. The War Department did not see fit to reimburse the company for the losses. This was the first in a series of disasters.

After gold was discovered in Colorado, Russell and John S. Jones decided to lay out a new road and establish a fast stage line from Leavenworth, straight west to Denver. They named the new enterprise Leavenworth and Pike's Peak Express Company. No one could accuse Russell of thinking in modest terms. He ordered fifty special red coaches and some 800 mules to stock the line. The advertised plan was that two Concord coaches pulled by four fast mules each, would leave Leavenworth and Denver each day. The $125 fare included excellent meals and sleeping accommodations.

The first coaches left Leavenworth April 18, 1859. Libeus Barney described the trip. He found the "excellent" meals, not quite as advertised, and the sleeping on the floor of an Indian tepee less than splendid accommodations. All along the road, livestock and people were suffering from the lack of water and provisions. At the end of ninety days, the line was bankrupt. Russell persuaded Major and Waddell to bail them out, lest this failure reflect on the integrity of the great freighting firm.

In late June, without regard to the tremendous loss of materials, Russell moved the stage line to St. Joseph, extended the line to Salt Lake City along the Oregon Trail with a branch line going to Denver from that route.

But this did not satisfy his ambitions. Although the freighting company was having contract troubles with the government, Russell now wanted a government contract to carry the mail from the Missouri River to California.

Even then mail contracts were political footballs. Citizens in California and in the northwest were clamoring for better communication with the East. A transcontinental mail contract had been awarded to John Butterfield. This route, however, went to California by the way of Santa Fe.

The erratic decisions made by the postal department made it almost impossible for Hockaday to fulfill his contract to carry mail from the Missouri River to Salt Lake City. They had also added the "last straw" to poor old

51

Chorpenning's burden to get mail from Salt Lake City to California. Russell reasoned that if he could prove to the easterners that mail could move over the Central Route (Platte Valley Road); if he could buy up Hockaday and Chorpenning contracts, he might be able to land a juicy government contract when Butterfield's contract expired. Now all he needed to do was to hold off his creditors, influence the present contract holders, pressure his friends in Washington and he could have his fortune secure.

Sometime during 1859, he decided again on his own that a fast relay postal service would be just the method to prove the advantages of the shorter Central route than Butterfield's.

While he was still dreaming about fast horses, young riders, and mail pouches, word came that the firm had suffered another disaster. When the supply trains had unloaded at Camp Floyd, Utah, the agent there selected 3500 of the best oxen for sale in California in the spring. Jackson Cooper was sent to take this herd to Ruby Valley, about one hundred miles south of what is now known as Elko, Nevada. On his way he was caught in a severe blizzard. When he finally reached the valley, snow was drifted so high that the animals could not find pasture. By Christmas, half were dead, and only two hundred were left by spring. This loss was estimated at $150,000.

What a shock it must have been to Majors and Waddell when Russell's son received a telegram on January 27, 1860 announcing his father's decision to begin the relay, a Pony Express, on April 3 of that year. Certainly the partners must have discussed such a venture before Russell had gone back to Washington. Majors in his book *Seventy Years on the Frontier,* said they reluctantly agreed to go along with the project because Russell had already given his promise to Senator Gwin, who was at that time serving as chairman of the Senate Post Office and Post Roads Committees. How could they possibly put together horses, men, and material to do this impossible task in just sixty-five days?

The mood of the country accepted speculation. No one knew how deeply in debt the company was. So again using their reputation as collateral, their leadership in attracting competent men, and their own abilities to organize, they began.

The first knowledge that the ranchers had, along the trail, was a small news article in the *Nebraska City News*. It read:

"Colonel Russell completed arrangements for a pony express from St. Joseph to the eastern terminus of Col. Bee's telegraph, and the first express leaves each end of the line on the third of April next to make the distance in ten days. The government has nothing to do with the enterprise. It is entirely private energy and capital. There will be eighty stations twenty-five miles apart. Horses and riders are now being placed."

The weather was bitter cold, but there had been very little rain or snow, so crews of workmen were sent out along the 1966 mile route. The route had been divided into five divisions. A. E. Lewis took charge of the first division from St. Joseph to Fort Kearny; Joseph A. Slade, the next stretch to Horseshoe Station; the third, to Salt Lake City, was bossed by James E. Bromley; Howard Egan took over, west to Robert's Creek; and the last division to Sacramento, was Bolivar Robert's responsibility. All were able men. Each man was familiar with his portion of the route, and was given absolute authority as long as he met the standards outlined by Russell, to whom they were all directly responsible.

Newspapers carried the often quoted advertisement:

WANTED Young, skinny, wiry fellows, not over eighteen. Must be expert riders, willing to risk death daily. Orphans preferred. Wages $25 per week.

Scores of young men rode into St. Joseph, Fort Kearny, Horseshoe Station, above Fort Laramie; to Salt Lake City; and to Carson City where the superintendents' headquarters were.

It was sometime in March 1860 that William Campbell and his brother John stopped at the Gilman ranch. These good friends from Nebraska City had been employed by

Russell to build new stations along the route. Billy, as his friends called him, later mentioned this trip. He said,

"The only jobs we could get—being what we were, husky farm lads, with empty pockets and a fair share of wits and a good knowledge of stock—were as teamsters with the great freighting firm of Russell, Majors, and Waddell. Their wagons covered the plains.

"It was the next year, 1860, that my first big chance came. That spring John (his brother) and I had been sent up by the company to the Platte country to work on building stations for the new freight and stage lines to Denver, where the mines had just opened.

"When we got up to Cottonwood Springs, Charlie White, the station keeper, said,

'There's going to be a fast mail service to California from St. Joe by horseback riders. Why don't you put in for it?' "

Billy knew that he had a good reputation for being an expert rider, so he applied. "They turned me down at first. They wanted strong lads of one hundred to one hundred twenty pounds at the most, whereas, I weighed one hundred forty pounds, which wasn't much for a six-footer. But they had a place for me soon. Many of the first boys quit or were worn out."

When Joseph A. Slade, boss of the division, stopped at the Gilman ranch to make arrangements for the pony relay station, the men about the ranch were impressed with this businessman who got things done. (He was sober on this trip.)

The Gilman station was a "swing" station. Here relief horses would be cared for, saddled, and made ready for the quick exchange of rider and mochilla as the mail moved swiftly along the Trail. Cottonwood Springs was designated as a home station. The rider would pass his precious cargo to another rider. After a few days of rest, the carrier would relieve the eastbound rider and pass the ranch again.

The stretch between Fort Kearny and the Crossing of the South Platte River was already well provided with stations. When Russell moved the stage line in late June

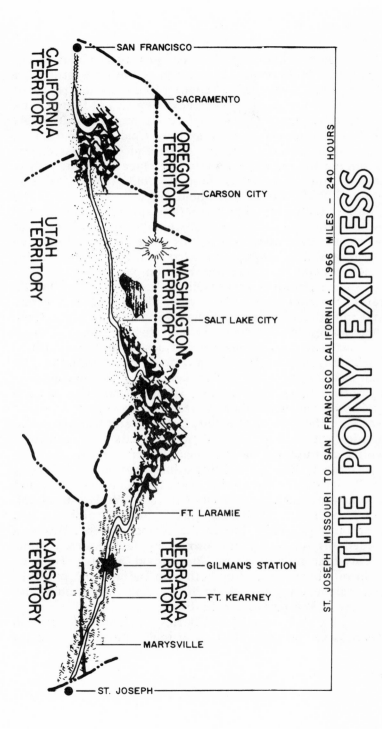

1859 crude stations had been provided about every twenty-five miles or so. About seventeen miles west of Fort Kearny (near Sydenham's ranch) a swing station provided fresh mules for the stage. The next stop was at Plum Creek where provisions were made to feed the stage passengers. At Willow Island (Mullally's) and at Cold Water (Smith, Peniston, Miller's) opportunities were given for passengers to sample the pilgrim whiskey. The stage company built a station some five miles beyond Cold Water (Midway Station). This station was about fifteen miles east of the Gilman ranch. Sometime during the spring of 1859 Daniel Smith, who had an interest in Cold Water, built another ranch just five miles west of this stage station. When the Western Stage Company extended their line to Denver this ranch became a station for that company.

Some eight miles west of Gilman's, George Clark built a cabin. Seven or eight miles farther (depending on the ruts and mud holes) was Cottonwood Springs. By early 1860, there was quite a settlement around this area. Five miles on this east side of Cottonwood Springs, near the mouth of Snell Canyon, Sam Machett was doing business. Later that year Jacob Snell was a trader there. Possibly, Machett was there trading with the Indians. In the *Kansas City Journal of Commerce,* September 24, 1858, it was reported that he was with the firm of Machett, Lindsey, and Company and had left with a large stock of Indian goods and planned to winter at Lupton's old fort near Cherry Creek.

Isador P. Boyer was doing a lusty business specializing in "spirits" in his cabin near the Cottonwood camp grounds. Across a ravine east of Boyer's, William Bischopf, and two French partners—Vilantry and Gardipi—built a ranch in April 1859, but in the spring of 1860, Bischopf traded his house for one owned by Jack Morrow some twenty-four miles west of Cottonwood Springs. Here he went into business trading both with Indians and pilgrims. His partners went back to Iowa. This new ranch also became a Western Stage Station.

In the fall of 1859, Charles McDonald, born in Tennessee, bought Dick Darling's partially finished building, completed it, stocked it, and on January 15, 1860 brought his lovely wife to the frontier. Mrs. McDonald was the first white woman to take up residence in Lincoln County. Charles McDonald had come to Nebraska Territory in 1855 and had settled for a time in Pawnee County.

There was a stage station about a mile and a half down the road from the McDonald's ranch. E. H. M. Patterson, traveling along the Trail, wrote in his diary on May 18, 1859:

> "Two miles further in Ash Creek—a dry run fringed with ash and box elder—where there is a trading house, a stage station, a dwelling, and a carpenter shop. These buildings are all constructed of cedar logs, procured from the ravines which furnish cedar logs of large size and in quantity."

Sheldon Davis, the New Hampshire friend, whom the Gilmans had followed to Iowa, then to Nebraska City, was the overseer of the Russell, Majors, and Waddell's supply depot here. Davis had married Margaret, James Fitchie's oldest daughter. Margaret also came out to be with her husband late in the summer. After the stations were completed, the Davises moved on farther west.

While all this building was going on, W. M. Hinman, a government employee, moved with his Indian wife, Clara, from Laramie. (He spent a short time at Fort Kearny before finally settling four miles west of Cottonwood Springs.) He brought a sawmill to the neighborhood. In a short time he fenced 250 acres of land. He planted a garden. The produce was especially popular with both Indians and travelers.

Early in the spring, Jack Morrow left his store in Kearny City, in charge of his partner, John Holland, and moved out to the flats some twelve miles west of Cottonwood Springs. (He was still advertising his store near Fort Kearny as late as May 16, 1860, in the *Rocky Mountain News.*]

By June, when the census was taken, there were sixty-two people between Hinman's ranch four miles west of

Cottonwood and Gilmans, fifteen miles to the east of the village.

The month of March was by far the busiest that the Gilmans had ever known. Wagons were rolling early that spring. Provisions were made to purchase two mowing machines for the hay promised to be an important commodity on the Trail.

Literally hundreds of wagons spread out for miles along the valley. The Majors' trains brought supplies, grain and fast horses to supply the express station. The Byram brothers from Nebraska City stopped their long train to renew acquaintances. They were moving a $20,000 cargo of government supplies to Denver. The men were surprised to see a train headed by a woman. Mrs. Grant from Washington County, Iowa, headed up twelve wagons going to take supplies to her husband at the mines.

The tempo increased at the ranch in April. Any transient looking for work was hired on the spot. The Trail became wider, dustier, and filled with ruts as stagecoaches dashed along, and freight wagons furrowed the tender sod of the valley. Russell did achieve the impossible. The ponies left St. Joe on schedule. For the next eighteen months those clattering hoofs continued to pound the Trail with but few interruptions, keeping a schedule through rain, hail, blizzards, and sweltering heat. Neither hostile Indians nor road agents could force these young men to surrender their precious cargo.

Those working at the Gilman ranch never seemed to tire of the excitement watching for that dashing courier. From November 1860 until its demise, Billy Campbell rode from Cottonwood Springs to the home station beyond Fort Kearny and back again. While he was resting between rides, he frequently caught a ride down to the Gilmans. Sam Fitchie, another Otoe County friend, tried hard to become a rider, but settled for a job, gathering the ponies that became lame or "used up" on this division, and replaced them with fresh, sound horses. Years later both of these men would retell the humorous incidents of the Trail around a Gilman or Fitchie family table.

Travelers experienced the usual changeable weather but no one anticipated the freak blizzard that decended on the plains late in the season. There was a loss of life both of men and animals before the sun shone again.

By May the Gilman store was well organized. Although it was still in a sod house, the shelves were neatly arranged with the merchandise that Jerry had brought from Nebraska City. Sacks of flour and of beans were neatly stacked behind a counter, made of a carefully hewn log. On the counter, was the small scales used in estimating the value of gold dust, which was often used as legal tender by those returning from the mines. The crude table and stools were also fashioned from the red cedar logs. There was a fireplace at one end for heat, but a fine iron cook stove had been hauled out from Nebraska City. In one corner, a pile of buffalo robes awaited a buyer.

One day when John was tending the store, he had an unusual visitor. He turned, as he heard someone stumble through the door. A tall, bronzed native with hair cut like a Sioux, wearing only a dirty breech cloth, staggered against the counter. He showed John an ugly black wound near his collarbone and motioned for a drink of water. Before John could get the water, the Indian collapsed on the floor.

The men moved the Indian, who seemed burning with fever, to one of the other soddies. They cleaned the wound and placed a tobacco poultice on the infected area. One of the boys had a pouch of herbs that an old squaw had given him when he had cut his foot with an ax the previous winter. They made a tea from the herbs and poured it down the sick man's throat. It was a day or two before the Indian regained consciousness.

The men around the ranch were divided into two camps. Some wanted to put an end to his misery, for the only "good Indians were dead Indians." But Gilmans were God-fearing men. They would not allow a hired man to beat a horse. Surely an Indian was better than a horse. No one could accuse them of being pious, but any stray animal or man could find a shelter at Gilmans. Travelers who stopped

59

wondered about this half-Sioux, half-Cheyenne Indian who seemed to attach himself to this trading post.

When he regained his strength, he disappeared. The cook rejoiced that there was one less to feed, especially this mouth that cleaned up everything in sight once he regained his appetite. But they were to see this Indian again and would be well paid for their kindness!

By June, the trail was clotted with wagons, horses, mules and people. *The Nebraska City Press* continued to advertise that the best "route to the gold fields" began at Nebraska City. The Omaha newspapers were just as certain that Omaha was the best jumping off place. Ranchers placed advertisements in the Omaha papers, and the *Rocky Mountain News* assuring the miners that supplies were available along the Trail.

On Saturday, June 2, Mollie Sanford, the 1857 diarist, with her husband and others in their party, stopped at the ranch. They had left Nebraska City and were destined for Denver. There seemed to be a fraternal feeling among those who had spent some time in Nebraska City, for Mollie wrote that night:

> Passed an Indian village this afternoon. The creatures looked too filthy to live. They are dreadful beggars and if they cannot get what they ask for, will steal. Stopped awhile at the Gilman ranch, a Nebraska City man. They live in an adobe house but have a splendid well of water, and I think more of that than I would of seeing a mansion.

The visitors brought all kinds of news to the lonely ranchers. They brought news of friends and of the latest gossip. It was the first time that they had heard about the great fire that had burned forty-one buildings in Nebraska City. The fire originated in a butcher shop south of Hawke's store. The loss had been estimated as over $100,000.

By June civilization began to catch up with those along the Trail. The area around Cottonwood Springs was to be organized into a county, and governing officers were to be elected. Because permanent settlers were few, only five men showed up for the election. The county was to be known as Shorter County (no one seemed to know why). The county seat was, of course, Cottonwood Springs. The following officers were elected:

Commissioners: I. P. Boyer, J. C. Gilman, and J. A. Morrow
County Judge: Charles McDonald
Treasurer: W. M. Hinman

The new officers were also advised that the census would be taken sometime during June.

THE CASE OF THE DRIED EARS

Summertime and the dry prairie brought a fear of prairie fires. People who camped at the campground on the little stream just east of the ranch kept a watch for that cloud which might appear up in the canyons or down the valley floor.

However, a different kind of "prairie fire" raged along the Trail from Upper California Crossing. It spread from wagon train to wagon train; from campground to campground; and on to the ranches along the way. Many versions of the story were told and continue to be told. There are always three factors involved in every story. The case of two dried ears, Jack Slade, the division superintendent of the Central Overland California and Pike's Peak Express Company, and Jules Beni, the French Canadian rancher and former division agent or at least the representative of the company stationed near Upper California Crossing.

Jules Beni had been engaged as an agent for the Overland Express possibly because he had built a ranch at this strategic crossing of the South Platte River. He had also been an employee of the old Hockaday line that had the mail contract.

Jules' ranch had a big square home station for the stage

61

company. There were also a hay barn, repair shops, a stable, and a corral for many head of stock and for the pilgrim trade. Most travelers agreed that Beni was a thief, a liar, and a braggart. He ruled the division like a tyrant. Passengers complained that he overcharged them for meals and lodging. Some were certain that he used stock and hay belonging to the company to supply his own ranch. Rumor had it, that he headed the gang which ran off stock along the Trail, and then sold the stock back to the desperate pilgrims.

When Ben Ficklin, the over-all director of the New Pony Express and Stage line, inspected the line, he was appalled to hear that this character employed by Russell, Majors, and Waddell had such a reputation. He ordered him replaced.

J. A. Slade had also built up a reputation. He was the son of William Slade, a Virginian who had founded Carlyle, Illinois. Slade's mother was the daughter of a wealthy landowner. Some time before Joe reached 21, he accidently killed a man. His family helped him to escape to the West. He enlisted and served in the army during the war with Mexico.

Slade, deep-chested and wiry, turned to freighting after the war. In 1857, when a Russell, Majors, and Waddell freighting train was camped near Green River, Wyoming, Slade, the wagon boss, drank himself into a fighting mood. In an argument with one of the drivers, Slade shot the driver. This was the first recorded murder on the Trail attributed to Slade. There were to be many more before his career ended.

In the next three years, Slade became the Paul Bunyan of the Overland Trail. Men called him Jack now. He was the champion of tall tale tellers; an inveterate drinker, and a lover of "hell-raisin'," but as a freighter he could roll wagons on schedule in spite of Indians, sore-footed stock or broken wagon wheels.

Early in 1860 Slade decided to replace Beni. The stock tenders warned Slade that Jules had promised to "get" Slade for replacing him. Others said that Slade had vowed to clean out all the horse thieves and other scoundrels on his division. Some said the confrontation took place when Slade appeared to take over his responsibilities; others said that Slade had found stock with the O. M. brand in Jules' corral. Anyway, they met. Slade, sober and unarmed, was greeted with a blast from Jules' shotgun. (One report was that seven buckshot were removed from Slade's body but he carried six shots for the rest of his life.) Slade's companions gathered him up and got him to a hospital in St. Louis (or was it Denver?) where he regained his health.

At the very time that Jules had shot Slade, Ben Ficklin, returning from his inspection trip, stopped at the station. When he was told what happened, he ordered Jules hanged.

Now again the story varies according to the narrator. Rough hands did tie the noose around Jules' neck, and he was hoisted up by a rope thrown over a tall corral gate. Some said that Ficklin permitted him to be raised and lowered until he was nearly strangled, then allowed him to be freed with the admonition to leave the country. Others were more dramatic and said that Jules' men cut him down and restored him after Ficklin had left. But at least Jules did not die from hanging.

After Slade's recovery he returned to his division. According to the code of the West, the score was not settled. One version said that Ben Holladay, who later would take over the Overland Mail, advised Slade that he would not have the respect of those on the Trail until he had done away with Jules. Others said that while he was recuperating, Slade planned how he would eliminate Beni.

Word came to Slade that Jules was in the area again, and when Slade stopped at Fort Laramie, he heard that Jules was at Bordeaux' ranch a short distance east of Laramie. Slade sent four men to capture him and make him a prisoner. Slade's men followed Jules to Chansau's ranch, captured him, bound him hand and foot and placed him at the rear of the station. Slade came on the next stage. When he saw his old enemy, Slade shot Jules through the mouth, then put a bullet through his head. When he was dead, Slade cut off his ears and carried them with him as a reminder to anyone who dared to challenge Slade's authority. Eugene Ware stated that a man who had known Jules for several years said that Jules had once killed two persons and that he had carried their four ears in his pocket! (Dr. C. G. Coutant wrote that Slade went back to Laramie and turned himself in, but his case was dismissed.)

An interesting version of the story appeared in a D.A.R. publication published in 1916 entitled *Nebraska Pioneer Reminiscences*. Mrs. Harriet McMurphy told the story of Ellen Addie Keyou. Addie was traveling with her family to California in 1857. When they stopped at Jules' ranch, Jules was attracted to the fourteen-year-old girl. He convinced her family that if he could have her for his wife he would take good care of her. She said they were secretly married. He was fatherly, protecting, and good-hearted to her. He hired a couple to do all the housework, and she traveled about with Jules. She had been convinced that Jules had paid Slade's hospital bill and that they had come to an understanding.

On the day that Slade shot Jules, Jules had gone without his wife to take cattle from one ranch to another. Pete Kozzoo, one of Jules' men, came galloping back, described what had happened to Jules. She and some of the ranch help fled to Denver. Jules had told her that he had money in a Denver bank, but she could not locate it. (Remembering how very new Denver was, it is not surprising.) She did find her family and returned to Decatur, a small Missouri River settlement. (The story did not say where she found her family.)

She married a Billy Becksted, who committed suicide near Bellevue. She then married his brother Elton, and when the book was published (1916) she still lived in a little cabin among the hills near Bellevue.

Some said that Slade was never the same man after this incident. He was constantly on the Trail. Ranchers accused of harboring horse thieves were burned out or forced to leave the country. Suspicious persons, Indians and ranchers all felt the fury of "Captain" Slade, as he now called himself. Few dared to question his authority. Efficiency ruled the business from Jules' ranch to Red Buttes, where he established his headquarters. But Slade's story is not finished here. His love of whiskey, and its influence upon the man would write the final chapter in 1864.

* * *

WHO WAS JOHNNY McBRIDE?

Sometime during this summer a boy calling himself Johnny McBride became part of the ranch family. Was he an "orphan of the Trail," another runaway from home, or had he attached himself to the wagon train to seek his fortune in the west? No one bothered to explain. It was not unusual for children or young people to become wards of ranchers or wagon trains. They were often treated as pets, and were targets for many practical jokes. Even Jack Slade took the son of a man whom he had killed and cared for him as though he were his own. Johnny was always characterized as fiercely loyal to the Gilmans and to their enterprises, not always wise in his defense of them.

Dr. C. M. Clark in his book *A Trip to Pike's Peak and Notes along the Way,* related an incident at Gilman's ranch which illustrates Johnny's attempt to "hold down the fort."

As we journeyed from our last encampment, we fell into into company with a Mr. R. and wife, who had a company of 18 persons whom they were boarding through to Denver. We reached Gilman's ranch, distance some 17 miles from Smith's where we instituted inquiries regarding wood, and were told that there was no wood to be had on the river for many miles. Some of us noticed timber a few miles distant, but not knowing whether it was situated on this side of the river or on an island we asked the question. There was a large load of cedar wood standing near that had just been hauled from the bluffs and the company purhcased a few sticks paying at the rate of two shillings per stick. While negotiating, Mr. R. jokingly remarked that he had a sufficient company to draw that load off. An employee of the ranch standing near, who probably was not accustomed to taking things in the 'Pickwickian' sense, immediately bristled up and says—'No, I be d----d if you have. If you think you have, I would just like to see you at it!

'Well, I have,' says Mr. R., 'but I did not wish it understood that I intended to take it without consent.'

'Well, stranger,' said the man, 'it won't do to talk so in this country; remember, you are not in the States.'

This sentiment aroused the feelings of the company, some of whom spoke in no flattering terms of the man's character. After a little bantering, he proceeded into the house and soon emerged with a revolver, thinking, no doubt, to frighten the pilgrims.

'My friend,' said one of the party, 'do you intend using that? I hardly think it would be healthy for you; we are a pretty strong party, and well armed.'

'Well, I believe I could pick off some of you before you had much chance,' spoke the fellow.

'You'd better try it, and we'll annihilate you and this shanty,' said some of the party whose looks and actions were so threatening that the fellow finally wilted and sloped back under cover, and we started on and encamped about a mile and a half beyond, where we found plenty of good wood, thus proving the fellow a liar, as well as a coward. Some of the party had a mind to go back and make an example of the chap, but were at length persuaded from the inglorious undertaking."

*　　*　　*

Although the Gilman ranch was not an official stage stop at this time, many stage coaches stopped to give their passengers a cool drink from the iron pump and to water the horses during these hot and dry August days. S. F. Nuckolls, the merchant from Nebraska City, stopped and chatted for a while. He had just sent eight wagons to O'Fallon's Bluff and Denver. He said that he and his partner Hawke had established a store and a sawmill near Denver. They also were sending a quartz mill.

Some time during this late summer a Russell, Majors,

and Waddell train camped for the night near the ranch. Among the stock tenders, there was a handsome Kansas boy. Young Bill Cody said that he had worked for the company since he was nine years old. Lew Simpson had taken him to Salt Lake City in 1857 when they were transporting supplies for General Albert S. Johnston. On their way back to Leavenworth they were ambushed by Indians near Plum Creek, and Bill killed his first Indian.

Later, this same Bill stopped on his way back to Kansas. This time he told of having ridden Pony Express on the Bill Trotter division, forty-five miles west of Jules' ranch.

Next year, when George Crisman, the leading wagonmaster for Russell, Majors, and Waddell, had purchased the old Jules ranch and was agent for the Pony Express, he encouraged Bill to ride again. He rode this time from Red Buttes on the North Platte River to Three Crossings on the Sweetwater—a short run of seventy-six miles. But circumstances would make him a contender for one of the longest rides of the Pony Express.

The Pony Express, its horses and riders were still the main topic of conversation. As the summer schedule continued, trouble mounted for the riders. They were often late arriving at the ranch. There had been an Indian attack in the Egan Canyon. A skirmish between Lieutenant Perkins and the Bannocks resulted in the death of seventeen Indians, and three soldiers were wounded. There had been battles between the Indians and Whites near Salt Lake City and Carson City during the summer. In May the Indians chased all the men from stations between Diamond Springs and Carson Valley. Armed guards were recruited and the stations resupplied.

Many riders were quitting and going back to civilization. Billy Campbell was given his chance to ride. Here is a portion of his story as told to his nephew, Sheldon Davis:

I rode from November 1, 1860 to October of the following year. Many quit rather than ride in winter both because of weather conditions and on account of it being a lonesome job. In the summertime the trail was thick with freight wagons, prairie schooners, and emigrants going to the mines and things were lively, but in winter this westward trek stopped.

On my first trip I faced a heavy snow storm all night and was nearly blind for several days. I was pretty well used up but recovered after a few days' rest.

My route covered a distance of seventy-five miles and was from Cottonwood Springs, later known as Fort McPherson to Lowell, seven miles below Fort Kearny. The longest ride I made at one time was 145 miles in fifteen hours but the hardest ride I ever made was from Fort Kearny to Big Sandy near Fairbury—130 with snow two and a half feet deep on the level and the ravines drifted full. It was bitter cold and I rode four different horses being twenty-four hours in the saddle. After that ride I was as badly used up as the horses.

We carried about twenty pounds of express and the company charged $5.00 per letter for one-half ounce written on tissue waterproof paper.

Abraham Lincoln had been elected in the fall of 1860 and with a war impending there naturally was great interest in his policies, his first message and what it would contain. Our schedule was ten miles per hour but when we carried his message we made fifteen miles per hour and cut the trip to California down to seven days and eighteen hours. And we killed several horses in doing it. The news of the bombardment of Sumter was carried across in eight days and nineteen hours.

In the fall of 1860 the telegraph line had been extended to Fort Kearney (Kearny) which was about 200 miles west of Omaha. It was there that we got our messages to take west and delivered messages from Sacramento. The telegrams were sealed and not to be opened until they arrived at Sacramento, but the operator at Kearney was an agreeable young man and told us all the news so we could spread it verbally among all the eager people along our route.

Although I had experiences with the Indians when I was teaming before and after the days of the express, I was never attacked during the period that I rode as a courier.

William Campbell's Colt revolver carried on the Pony Express. Left: Harold H. Gilman (Jeremiah's grandson) Associate Professor, University of Nebraska. Right: Paul R. Jenkins, Director, Pony Express Rerun 1967, Gothenburg, Nebraska.

We frequently had amusing experiences on our trips. One night I was riding a mule and fell asleep. When I was awakened I was nearer to the station I had just left as the mule had turned around and gone back. On another dark night I became lost and could not find my way until I reached the Platte River when I oriented myself by finding the way the water was flowing.

TWO FACE RETURNS

No one had seen nor heard from the Indian which the Gilmans had cared for in the early summer. Some of the old squawmen insisted that it had been Two Face himself who had become a legend among both the Sioux and Cheyenne as being a brave warrior and a cunning trader. Late in October he came galloping up to the trading post on a fine Sioux pony. Thrown across the shoulders of the pony was a roll of beautiful buffalo robes, soft and silky to touch. Each was carefully lined with red flannel. Two Face had brought merchandise that could not be bought from the Indians who hung around the ranches to trade robes for trinkets or tobacco.

Jerry Gilman had learned by watching the Sioux in nearby camps that gift-giving was an important ceremony for the Sioux. So all the men gathered around, while with elaborate gestures, Two Face laid the robes before the Gilmans with a salutation, "Cola," which meant "friend." The brothers accepted the gift with appropriate ceremony. Then they all drank the coffee that the cook had prepared for their lunch.

Like most traders on the trail, the Gilmans succeeded because they were opportunists. So, seeking the excellence of the robes and the profits to be made by trading with tribes who were not trail beggars, they entered into a business arrangement with Two Face to act as trader for them with bands far from the Trail. They entrusted him with quantities of trading goods: brown sugar, tobacco, red calico, and trinkets. He again disappeared over the prairie. Would they ever see him again?

THE YEAR ENDS

When the work at the ranch tapered off, the extra help was paid and sent on their way. John Gilman, dressed in "store clothes," hailed an eastbound stage as it approached the ranch. He carried a leather "satchel" which was heavy from the quantity of gold dust and coin which he was taking with him to meet their obligations in Nebraska City.

It was a beautiful December day. The sun shone but the air was clear and cold. The coach, its well-seasoned white oak body once painted red, now was covered with a thick layer of dust. John could see that there were already five passengers in the coach, so, not wishing to crowd his big frame onto the narrow seat, especially since he was wearing two guns, he climbed up beside the driver. After a few minutes' rest the driver cracked his whip and called out to his four mules and the team lunged off down the Trail. The valley was brown, spotted with bits of snow left after a recent snow shower. Here and there the bleaching bones of buffalo gleamed in the sunlight. John had visited with this driver on several occasions when he had been up at Cottonwood Springs, but now the driver, proud of his skill, devoted all his attention to getting the stage through on time.

John had plenty of time to think as the coach jolted and swayed over the frozen trail. The stops to change teams were welcome to the travelers as they could get down and walk around to relieve their tired muscles. A friendly bottle of "spirits" was passed around before they climbed back into the cumbersome vehicle. The last issue of the *Nebraska City News* had listed a letter for him at the post office. He wondered if it could be a letter from his mother back in New Hampshire. He also made elaborate plans for his week in Nebraska City.

The week that he planned to stay in the city was far too short. He spent the time discussing plans for a freighting outfit to carry merchandise to Denver and perhaps to Salt Lake City in the spring. Hawke and Nuckolls promised him all the freight that he could carry. He managed to stop at

71

George Crater's bathing room almost every day for a warm bath. For twenty-five cents a man could know the luxury of a hot bath!

John spent most of his evenings at the James Fitchie home. Hiring a riding horse from the old stable he had once owned, he would travel to the Fitchie farm some nine miles south on what was known as Camp Creek. The Fitchies had been some of the first friends that he had made when he had come to Nebraska. James and Elizabeth Fitchie had been reared in Ireland, and came to America soon after they were married. Since Fitchie was a carpenter, he had less trouble finding work, first in Pennsylvania, then Iowa, before coming to Nebraska, than most immigrants.

The Fitchies had known the hard times that most of the first Nebraska settlers had known. James loved to tell about the oldest daughter's wedding, one of the first in Nebraska City. When she had married Sheldon Davis (The same Sheldon Davis who had been in Iowa and later at Box Elder just west of Cottonwood Springs) it was bitter cold. There were no eggs and very little sugar and flour to make the wedding cake! But John had other reasons for coming to the Fitchies than to listen to James' Irish stories. Fitchie had three beautiful daughters still at home. He had special eyes for Martha, Mat, her family called her. Her hair was dark and curly, and her dark eyes were seldom serious. Her Irish tongue could tease and John found a match for his quick wit. When the neighbors gathered to dance the squares, Martha's tiny feet scarcely touched the floor. Yes, the week went too fast for John Gilman!

Chapter V

1861
"LOOSED LIGHTNING"

When John Gilman returned from Nebraska City, he was surprised and delighted that Two Face had come in with more robes, moccasins, rawhide whips, and halters made by the Sioux or Cheyenne. (Since Two Face had families in both tribes, they were unable to tell where he had been trading.) Jerry and the others continued to cut and haul cedars from the canyon across the way. There were now enough cedars to build a fine new trading post and large corrals to accommodate more pilgrims when the heavy traffic began in the spring.

In the evenings after the day's work was completed, the men filled their pipes with good smoking tobacco and John related the news and gossip which he had heard in the city. Politics were now of special interest even to those out of the states. Jerry, still loyal to his old New Hampshire rearing, took issue with John's opinions, for John had been converted to the Democratic party. The discussions were lively, and filled with Yankee wit.

But sober events had happened and were happening. South Carolina had adopted the Ordinances of Secession on December 20, 1860. It was rumored that Mississippi, Florida, Alabama, Louisiana, Georgia and Texas would soon follow. Many young "hot bloods" were all ready to enlist, and someone had reported that Samuel W. Black,

73

territorial governor of Nebraska, might resign to recruit a regiment of Pennsylvania volunteers. Most people agreed that if there were a war, it would not last long. Much would depend upon that A. Lincoln from Illinois who had been elected president.

But Washington was still far away. They were more interested in discussing plans for the new ranch buildings, and for the outfitting of two big trains that would not only bring supplies to the ranch but would travel on to Denver.

It is fair to guess that the vehicles and other equipment for these wagon trains were accumulated rather than purchased all at one time. Wagons, especially the best ones made in St. Louis by Joseph Murphy, were expensive.

These wagons were larger than the old immigrant wagons. The bed was sixteen feet long and six feet high. The rear wheels were seven feet in diameter. The frame or running gear was supported by front and rear axles. Cast iron cups were fitted over the ends of the wooden axles and the wheels turned round the cups. (Each wheel had to be greased daily with a mixture of tar, resin, and tallow.) Most freight wagons had six or eight bows, semicircles of pliable wood attached at each end to the sides of the wagon, making a skeleton for a tent-like top. The bows were covered by two layers of coarse linen cloth called osnaberg. There was a long box attached to the back of the wagon box, which served many purposes. It carried fuel on the trail and served as a feed trough when in camp. The front of the wagon was closed by a canvas so the wind would not catch it and overturn the wagon. (The bullwhacker never rode in the wagon.)

Since Gilmans had been hauling their own supplies from Nebraska City since they had been on the Trail, they knew dealers, and they also knew how one might obtain equipment by keeping a shrewd eye out for bargains. Many discouraged pilgrims would sell their outfit for much less than purchase price just to get money to take them back to their old homes. Many small operators owed for their wagons and when they could not pay, dealers foreclosed on the mortgages. Dealers were eager to dispose of this second-handed property.

After the fall of Fort Sumter, soldiers had been recalled from western army posts, and there were sales of surplus army supplies. The Gilmans had acquired some excellent cattle for trading stock, so the animals were well fed and ready to work by the time the weather allowed the trains to roll.

The most important ingredient for any successful freighting enterprise was a man to act as wagon boss. If he were competent, and had reliable teamsters, the freight went through with a minimum of loss or trouble. Here again the Gilmans were lucky. Hank Clifford, who had been with them most of the time since they left Nebraska City, was eager to assume the responsibility. He had worked for Russell, Majors, and Waddell, knew most of the Nebraska City merchants, and could drive a hard bargain. This powerfully built young man had keen eyes which could "size" up a man or a situation. John Nelson said, "He knew everything about everybody's business."

The wagon boss had many responsibilities. He must know how to load a wagon properly, distributing the weight of the load so the center of gravity was as low as possible. Fragile or perishable items must be protected from shifting cargo. He must know where campsites and sources of water were. He was the defender of his train against all the hazards of the trail. Beyond responsibilities he needed certain skills, such as the ability to shoe an ox or repair a wagon, how to doctor a sick man or beast, and how to make quick decisions.

As important as these qualifications were, he must also be a leader—strong, brave, and tireless. He must be shrewd enough to understand and handle all kinds of men. He was often called upon to be both judge and jury. He must be a businessman keeping accurate accounts, for teamsters were allowed to purchase such items as combs or socks on credit, and this cost was subtracted from their wages at the end of the haul.

Cooking for a train crew was not simple. In some wagon

trains, the teamsters divided into messes and each teamster took his turn as cook. But Gilmans supplied a cook wagon for each train of twenty-five wagons. Perhaps well-fed men were more content, less trouble and more apt to stay with the train.

The cook wagon was a light wagon pulled by four horses or mules. It was topped with bows and a canvas cover to protect supplies and bed rolls. Fitted into the wagon box at the rear, was a chuck box. It was about four feet high. The front slanted and was hinged at the bottom. When it was let down, sturdy legs unfolded, and the cook had a work table. Inside the box were shelves and partitions holding tin plates, cups, knives, forks and other utensils for food preparation. The wagon itself was loaded with supplies to last the trip. It carried several kegs of water; a large container of flour with a fitted lid; coffee, and such staples as bacon, beans, rice, syrup, dried fruit, salt, sugar, soda, onions, potatoes, a keg of pickles, and a few tins of corn or tomatoes. In cool weather, there might be a cured ham or a side of beef. On the side of the wagon swayed a stone jug containing warm water thickened with flour, and sprinkled with a handful of sugar. This fermented and became the "sour dough" which was used as leavening for biscuits and hot cakes.

The cook wagon, traveling faster than the oxen and wagons, would go ahead of the train and stop at a prearranged camping place. There the cook would build a fire and prepare a hot meal. Most outfits ate only two meals. The first came about ten o'clock in the morning while the animals rested and the men checked the wagons. About two in the afternoon, the train would move again. They would travel until late afternoon or early evening when the cook would again provide the evening meal.

John Gilman's son reported that the Gilman brothers had two twenty-six wagon trains. But it is doubtful that their first venture into the long haul included the two trains. It is more likely that they began with one train and accumulated enough capital to operate the second.

The citizens of Nebraska City had not built the road

straight west to the Platte Valley which Alexander Majors had requested. R. M. Rolfe in a newspaper article (November 19, 1899) recalled that in 1861, Majors chose William E. Hill to go over the country and find a new route. There was a decent road to Saltillo (8 miles south of the present Lincoln), Salt Creek and the Blue River had been bridged, so Hill plowed a furrow straight west from Saltillo to the Platte Valley. The freighting wagons straddled the fullow and before the end of summer the new road had been established.

Both the Nebraska City newspaper and the Omaha paper advertised the roads to the gold fields. They mentioned ranches or camping grounds and estimated the distances along the trails. The new road from Nebraska City to Denver shortened the distance about fifty miles. But most of the freighters with big trains still traveled the old ox-bow road, because there were more farms and camping grounds along the way. (Gilmans were still traveling this route in 1862 according to J. Sterling Morton.)

Little has been recorded about the farms or ranches between Nebraska City and Fort Kearny on the Ox-bow route. However, as travelers approached Fort Kearny, these were mentioned: Newells, Newins, Bracketts, Harman and Biggs: Bissell and Earl; then Bissells (There were two Bissell brothers, Thompson and William, who had settled in Butler County in 1859). John McMechan (a surveyor in Nebraska City) said that it was 12 miles from Bissells to the Henchman ranch; 10 miles to the St. Louis Ranch; then the Elk Ranch was 7 miles farther; and Platte Valley House was three miles from Elk Ranch and 6 miles on to Fort Kearny.

But the ranches west from Fort Kearny continued to mushroom. In 1861 the following ranches were mentioned either by the Omaha or the Nebraska City newspapers. The distances between ranches varied. This was probably due to estimation made by different travelers at different times of year. There was little attempt to measure accurately, for most travelers were more interested in how long it would take them to travel.

Fort Kearny	Mileage

Kearny City 2
Francis Beerman's ranch 1
Eight Mile Point (Thomas Keeler) 6
Young and Co. 3-1/2
Central Overland California
    & Pike's Peak Express Station 3-1/2
    (This was called Shakespear the year before)
Sydenham's Ranch (Hopetown) 3-1/2
Iowa Ranch (Gardiner's) 3
Davidson's 3
25 Mile Ranch (Fred Smith) 3
Finley Burtch 4
Plum Creek (2 ranches, Louis Wiscamb and Thomas) ... 6
C.O.C. & P.P. Express Co. 1
James Parson 2
John Sharp (Blacksmith) 2
Freeman's Ranch 3
Ranch (Probably Mullally's) 9
Smith's East Ranch (Miller and Peniston also here)
    (A Western Stage Station) 9
C.O.C. & P.P. Ex. Station (Midway) 5
Smith's West Ranch 5
Gilman's..................................... 10
Clark—McDonald's 6
Capitola City (Machetts) 8
Cottonwood Springs
    (3 ranches—McDonald, Boyer and the buyer of
    Bischof's)................................. 1
C.O.C. & P.P. Ex. Station 1
Box Elder (Baldwin and Pegram) 2
Hays & Bro. 1
W. M. Hinman 1
Junction Ranch (Jack Morrow's) 2
Fremont Slough (Bishopf)
    (Western Stage Station) 11
Fremont Springs 9
C.O.C. & P.P. Express Station
O'Fallon's Bluff (Williams Ranch) 8

Fort Kearny	Mileage
Moore's Ranch (Western Stage Station)	3
Dorsey's (Dauchy)	2
C.O.C. & P.P. Ex. Co. Station	25
Diamond Springs C.O.C. & P.P. Express Station	25
Beauvais (Lower Platte Crossing)	3
Baker and Fales (Buckeye Ranch) (Western Stage Station)	2
Sand Creek Ranche (Walden & Horner) Julesburgh (Upper Crossing of South Platte R.) C.O.C. & P.P.	12
Nebraska Ranch (Ackley & Forbes) (Western Stage Station)	5
Twelve Mile Ranch (Simons & Hafford)	14
Spring Hill C.O.C. & P.P. Ex. Station	5
Lillian Springs (Western Stage Station)	21
C.O.C. & P.P. Express Station	21
H. Godfrey's	5
Steven and Moore Beaver Creek C.O.C. & P.P. Ex.	23
Wm. Mackin & Co.	2-1/2
Fred Lamb C.O.C. & P.P. Express Station	1/4
Bijou	13
C.O.C. & P.P. Express Station	15
Living Springs	13
Kiowa Ranch	5
Box Elder (Conant) C.O.C. & P.P. Express Station	9
Eight Mile Creek (Morris)	13
Denver	8

The ranches from Julesburg on would change even by the next year. Many were trying to find a better way across the dry sandy plains north and east of Denver.

While the Gilmans and their employees were carrying on with the business of running the road ranch and loading the transporting supplies to Denver, many changes were being made.

When the territory of Nebraska was organized in 1854, all the land between the Missouri River north of the fortieth parallel to the forty-ninth parallel, west of the Missouri

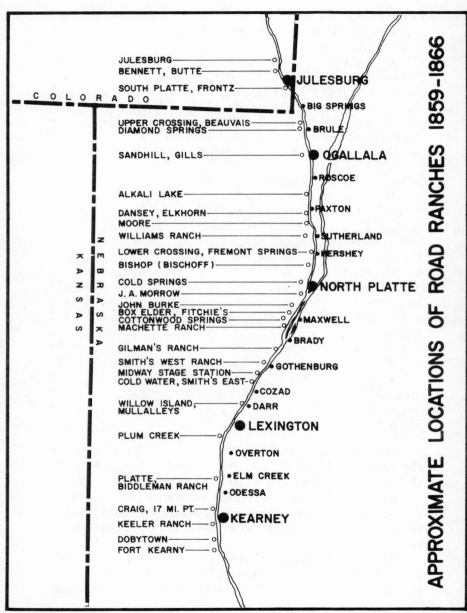

APPROXIMATE LOCATIONS OF ROAD RANCHES 1859-1866

JULESBURG
BENNETT, BUTTE
SOUTH PLATTE, FRONTZ
● JULESBURG

COLORADO

● BIG SPRINGS

UPPER CROSSING, BEAUVAIS
DIAMOND SPRINGS
● BRULE

SANDHILL, GILLS
● OGALLALA

● ROSCOE

ALKALI LAKE

DANSEY, ELKHORN
MOORE
● PAXTON

WILLIAMS RANCH
● SUTHERLAND

LOWER CROSSING, FREMONT SPRINGS
● HERSHEY

BISHOP (BISCHOFF)

COLD SPRINGS
J. A. MORROW
● NORTH PLATTE

JOHN BURKE
BOX ELDER, FITCHIE'S
COTTONWOOD SPRINGS
MACHETTE RANCH
● MAXWELL

GILMAN'S RANCH
● BRADY

SMITH'S WEST RANCH
MIDWAY STAGE STATION
COLD WATER, SMITH'S EAST
● GOTHENBURG

● COZAD

WILLOW ISLAND,
MULLALLEYS
● DARR

PLUM CREEK
● LEXINGTON

● OVERTON

PLATTE,
BIDDLEMAN RANCH
● ELM CREEK

● ODESSA

CRAIG, 17 MI. PT.
● KEARNEY

KEELER RANCH

DOBYTOWN
FORT KEARNY

NEBRASKA

KANSAS

Location of Road Ranches in Platte Valley 1859-1860

River to the Summit of the Rocky Mountains, was called Nebraska Territory. In February, 1861, Congress voted to chop off the northern part of Nebraska Territory and make it Dakota. They also voted to take a bite out of the southwest area, combine it with a portion of Kansas Territory and make the territory of Colorado.

The second change came about in the mail service. The Confederate troops had raided the Butterfield Overland Mail going to California by the way of Santa Fe, and the Indians had attacked a mail coach in the Apache Pass. Congress was debating at that time, a bill attempting to establish a daily mail from the Missouri River to California. An amendment to this postal bill switched the government subsidized Butterfield line to the Central Route (Along the Platte Valley road.) The Pony Express was required to continue until the transcontinental telegraph was completed. Russell's suggestion of the previous year to have a semi-weekly Pony Express run was part of the new plan. The Express must carry up to five pounds of government mail, free of charge. The public now paid only $1.00 per half ounce. For this daily mail service and more frequent Pony Express, the government would pay $1,000,000 a year plus a hundred thousand dollars to Butterfield for damages in the moving to the Central Route.

A deal was made between the Butterfield Company, and the Russell enterprises. The Western Stage Company, which operated a stage from Omaha to Denver, was paid to run the stage line from Omaha to Fort Kearny only. So at last the stage and express business from the Missouri River to California was under one management, but not William Russell's.

In April 1861 Russell resigned and the conglomerate was turned over to a prominent lawyer, Bela M. Hughes, a cousin of another promoter who was interested in transcontinental transportation, Ben Holladay.

Ben Holladay, a young Kentuckian, settled in Missouri in 1836. By 1861 he had made a name for himself on the frontier. He had freighted with old Sublette to Santa Fe; was a courier for Colonel Alexander Doniphan to the

Mormons when they were in Missouri. He had owned a store in Weston, Missouri, Alexander Major's home base. He had invented special wheels for freighting wagons that would improve travel over sand trails. He freighted to Salt Lake City; made money operating a distillery; succeeded in getting a herd of cattle from Utah to California. In 1861 he bought a steamship line. Also in 1861 he had what Russell, Majors and Waddell so badly needed—money.

Accounts differ as to the time when Holladay actually began to lend the great company money. But by June 1861 the sum was thought to be at least $70,000. On July 5, he demanded a mortgage on the stageline and equipment. By November he was given a bond for $400,000 and a three-year mortgage.

Holladay's long years of personal resentment and envy toward both Majors and Russell; his insatiable ambition; his gambler's compulsion to capitalize on the opportunity at hand, precipitated his impatience. By the end of December Ben declared the bond forfeit and moved for foreclosure.

The third event that effected the states and the frontier as well happened on March 4, when the tall, gaunt lawyer from Illinois was sworn in as the sixteenth president of the United States. One month and eight days later, Fort Sumter fell to the Confederacy and the long, bloody war began. The Nebraska City newspaper began almost immediately to criticize the new president. When in May the president called troops from the western forts to increase the army of the North, many ranchers began to worry about Indian troubles.

ARRIVAL OF JOHN YOUNG NELSON

In the book *Fifty Years on the Trail,* the life story of John Young Nelson as told to Harrington O'Reilly, Nelson describes his coming to work at the Gilman ranch. (O'Reilly, an English writer, was fascinated with John Nelson and his family when he appeared with Buffalo Bill and his Wild West show in England.)

Nelson said, "I was first undecided where to go, but remembering I had heard that two brothers named Gilman had just started a ranche about fifteen miles along the road towards the east, I went up there to see if they wanted any hands.

"These two men were twins named respectively, Jerry C. and John K. (Nelson was wrong about this. Although many people believed that John and Jerry were twins, John was five years older than Jerry. Jerry was a twin but his twin brother stayed in New Hampshire.) Their age was about thirty years, and both were tall men. John was a big, burly fellow, and Jerry as tall, but thin as a lath. They started one of the largest ranches along the road, and when I arrived were at work building the shanty, helped by six men, who were lumbering up logs.

"I made a trial engagement with them for one month. My duties were the same as at Billy Hill's and my pay fifteen dollars per month. This was small, but I knew it would soon increase.

"We had stabling for one hundred and seventy-five horses, and a large corral capable of holding any number of emigrants. Traffic was pretty brisk along the road just then, wagons were nearly always in sight, and thousands of emigrants were making their way to California.

"In a week or ten days we got shipshape, and business commenced in real earnest. At the end of the first month I received twenty-five dollars instead of fifteen and before the end of the third my pay had increased to sixty-five dollars per month. My value was not only in my aptitude for looking after the business generally; the Gilmans discovered that my knowledge of the Indian language was of use to them, and they were consequently, very anxious to keep me."

It was not long before the mouthy little squaw man had revealed his past to anyone who would listen. He said that he had run away from home, Malden, Virginia. He got tired of traveling with a wagon train headed west, so he joined Spotted Tail and his band, spending the next several years moving freely from tribal life back to white man's society.

He insisted that he had scouted for Brigham Young when the first Mormon expedition traveled the Platte Valley. He gave details concerning Gratton's massacre and General Harney's fight with Spotted Tail at Ash Hollow. He said that he had married and lost several squaws. He described how in 1857 Russell, Majors, and Waddell had hired him to accompany General Albert Johnston's expedition to Salt Lake City, witnessing the Mountain Meadow massacre. After many more hair-raising escapades he finally worked for Billy Hill, who had a ranch and ran the stage station two and one-half miles from Cottonwood Springs.

When Billy Hill was killed on a ferry boat near Omaha, Nelson rejoined the Brules, who were camped nearby. He married another Sioux girl. When he learned that her big family expected him to support them all, he escaped and found employment with the Gilmans.

*   *   *

The great stream of all kinds of vehicles which Nelson mentioned traveled the valley of the Platte River, on their way to California, Oregon or Colorado. When they left the Cold Water ranch the low range of hills to the south of the trail rose into a wall of canyon-scarred hills. By the time they had reached Midway and Smith's west ranch the valley narrowed into a wide, grassy corridor.

Long before they reached the Gilman ranch they could see the flag flying above this treeless oasis. The trail twisted along the loam shelf that separated the sandy marshland along the shallow banks of the Platte River from the flat valley floor.

The bluffs on the south side of the valley were more rugged now. The cedar trees shadowed the deep canyons that twisted up into the hills looking for the world like a sandpile where a giant had poked out the valley with his forefinger and left the rolling ridges along its border.

Just before the westbound wagons reached the big sod corral, which Nelson mentioned, a side trail branched right, leading to an old camp ground. Here a spring-fed stream emptied into the Platte River. The trail made an arch toward the river but the ranch site was still over a half mile from the shallow river bed. A grassy meadow separated the trail from the river.

One might stand in the doorway of the new cedar trading post, look over the iron pump, past the snubbing post where animals were tied for shoeing, and watch the caravans weaving their way along the hoof-packed highway.

Three small soddies huddled northwest of the store. Between the soddies and the trail was a sod structure sometimes a storehouse, sometimes a blacksmith shop. (The corral shown on the Sitgreaves map north of the trail was evidently built later. Comparing the size of the sod remains and the plat drawn in 1865 it would appear that this was the army post. Official records from the National Archives record that the army paid $1,825.83 for the rent of the ranch from October 3, 1864 to April 10, 1866.)

The Nebraska City newspapers brought items of special interest to the ranchers. Perhaps the news that the Byram brothers were taking over the Alexander Majors' contract for corn and supplies for the army post in the West was the first time that those on the Trail knew of the serious state of the Russell, Majors, and Waddell company. August Byram had long been a confidential agent for Majors, and his younger brother Peter had also worked for the big company. They were tied to the company by marriage, for William B. Waddell had married their sister, Susan Byram.

The May 25th issue carried Edward Creighton's announcement that the telegraph would begin by July to build westward from Fort Kearny. (Here was an opportunity to sell more cedar logs and John Gilman, who was always looking for opportunities, made plans to go to Omaha to meet Edward Creighton.)

Creighton, the son of Irish immigrants, had come to Omaha in 1856. He had married Miss Lucretia Wareham of Dayton, Ohio. Already he had amassed a fortune estimated at $25,000. He was the builder of telegraph lines.

While he was building the telegraph lines from St. Louis to Omaha, he dreamed of building a line to California. He

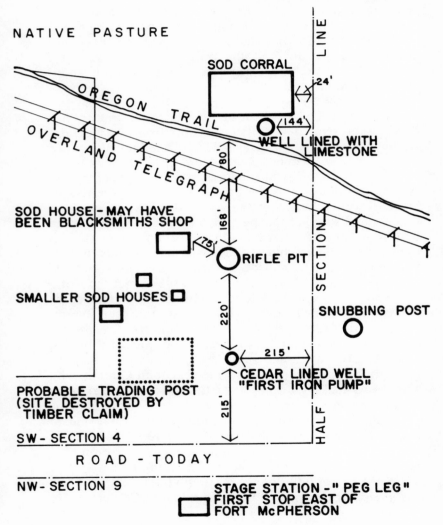

GILMAN'S STATION
IN PECKHAM PRECINCT

NATIVE PASTURE

OREGON TRAIL

OVERLAND TELEGRAPH

SOD CORRAL

24'

144'

WELL LINED WITH LIMESTONE

80'

168'

SOD HOUSE - MAY HAVE
BEEN BLACKSMITHS SHOP

75'

RIFLE PIT

SMALLER SOD HOUSES

220'

SNUBBING POST

215'

CEDAR LINED WELL
"FIRST IRON PUMP"

215'

PROBABLE TRADING POST
(SITE DESTROYED BY
TIMBER CLAIM)

SW - SECTION 4

ROAD - TODAY

NW - SECTION 9

LINE

SECTION

HALF

STAGE STATION - "PEG LEG"
FIRST STOP EAST OF
FORT McPHERSON

APPROXIMATE MEASUREMENTS BY HENRY H. STRICKLAND, SILVER CREEK, NEBR.

Site of Gilman road ranch

consulted Jeptha H. Wade of Cleveland, who was the best authority on telegraph systems. He corresponded with General Carpenter, president of the California State telegraph. This resulted in an agreement for Creighton to survey a route. Creighton left by stage late in 1860 for Salt Lake City. From there he traveled on mule back to Carson City during the bitter cold of January 1861.

Motivated by the $40,000 per year for ten years appropriated by Congress, Creighton formed a company and agreed to build westward from Fort Kearny to Salt Lake City by the way of Julesburg and South Pass. The California company would build eastward. A wager between the two companies, the first to Salt Lake City, made the project more exciting.

John Nelson, the squaw man who worked for Gilmans, commented:

> After I had been there about three months the telegraph line to California was commenced and the Gilmans secured the contract to furnish the telegraph poles. These were of cedar which grew abundantly in the canyons about five miles from the ranche.
>
> I had charge of eight men and some wagons. My duty was to lumber up these poles and pile them along the road in stacks. This job was usually finished about one o'clock, when my work commenced in the ranche, either attending to the emigrants or fixing drinks for the travelers.
>
> About twice a week, in my off time, I ran down to the Indian encampment to see my squaw and take her coffee, sugar, and other things. One day when I came home with a larger parcel of delicacies than usual, I found she had disappeared with a buck. It was the same old tale over again. Once more wifeless I had to face an unsympathetic and relentless world. Two or three drinks, however, straightened me, and I returned to my duties a greater woman-hater than ever.

Building the telegraph proceeded at a fantastic pace. It started at Fort Kearny on July 4 and was completed by October 24. But the construction of the poles and wire was only part of the task. To maintain the lines required ingenuity and at times the services of the cavalry.

Donald McNicol, at the forty-fifth reunion of the old time telegraphers in Omaha, September 1928, stated that 400 armed men, 100 head of beef cattle, 500 head of oxen and mules and over 100 wagons headed out from Fort Kearny and built five to six miles of line each day. Creighton required not less than twenty-five poles per mile. They used 'nigger-head' insulators—glass covered with wooden caps.

Many methods were used to discourage the Indians from tampering with the shining wires. A group of chiefs were told "bad medicine tales" and given electrical shocks. Perhaps the most effective deterrent came as a surprise even to the telegraph officials. A party of Indian braves near O'Fallons Bluff were encouraged by one of their number to challenge the black magic. So they chopped down a pole, cut the wire and proceeded to rip as much as the group could handle and take to their village. They cut about a half mile of wire. All the Indians on horseback, in single file, caught hold of the wire and pulled it across the prairie toward their encampment.

An electrical storm overtook them that hot summer day, and as they crossed a ridge, lightning found an excellent ground. All were knocked from their ponies and some were injured. They dropped the wire, and word spread rapidly that the wire did have magical powers. They did, however, continue to cut down poles for firewood. Later their interference greatly hampered communication.

Crews of repairmen frequently stopped at the Gilman ranch. Sloat and Holcomb were regular callers as they patrolled the line from Fort Kearny westward.

Just as there was national rejoicing over the completion of the telegraph, it sounded the end of the colorful Pony Express. Some eighty riders were out of work and a fleet of fine horses became surplus.

By the middle of September, the wagon trains returned from Denver; the hay had been cut, hauled and stacked near the corral and when the train went back to Nebraska

City for winter supplies almost all of the help went too. Nelson and Johnny McBride stayed to care for the stock and to provide for any stragglers that might be on the Trail so late in the season. Jerry arrived back at the ranch about the first of November. John Nelson set out on his expedition, now that he was no longer needed at the ranch. He said:

> During the winter I took a couple of waggons (wagons) and two teamsters for the Gilmans, to trade with the Indians on Big Turkey Creek, about one hundred and fifty miles away. There I found the Oglalas, Brules, and a few Cheyenne, and among them my old friends, Spotted Tail and Two Buck Elk. Spotted Tail had been released from prison and returned to his tribe. Both were glad to see me again, and I passed a very pleasant three months with them, returning to the ranche with the whole of my stock sold out and laden with a good supply of furs.
>
> I believe I had four hundred and seventy-five of the best buffalo robes alone, besides other skins, raw hide lariats, etc.
>
> The robes cost about one and a quarter dollar each and sold at four dollars. In addition, I had two thousand dried buffalo tongues, which I purchased for thirty-six cents a dozen and resold to the emigrants at twenty-four dollars a dozen.
>
> My first experiment in the trading line resulted in a very handsome profit to my employers. I shall never forget the look of astonishment on their faces when I counted out my treasures. They would hardly believe that I had done so well, and they made me a present of a horse, saddle, and a bridle, and raised my pay.

John Gilman did not walk beside the slow bull train when he returned to the ranch. On October 3, he was married to pretty Martha Fitchie in her parents' home on Camp Creek nine miles from Nebraska City. They drove the long road out to the ranch in a fine new buggy behind a matched span of thoroughbred horses. Everyone was delighted to see a pretty woman around the trading post. But to the Gilman brothers, who always enjoyed good food, her apple pie was the best treat on the prairie.

Chapter VI

1862

THE CRACK OF THE WHIP

While the monotonous life of the road ranches went on as usual, many changes were taking place in the country. The War between the States had not been completed in a few weeks as many had thought. The Nebraska volunteers had seen the horrors of war along the Mississippi River. Newspapers described a strange sea battle between an iron "cheesebox" on a raft and a wooden vessel. A man named Gatling had invented a new gun, able to fire 350 rounds of ammunition a minute. Governor Saunders of Nebraska Territory issued a proclamation establishing a state militia. Ordinary citizens conducted artillery practice in Nebraska City. President Lincoln signed the Homestead Act on May 20.

Every road ranch along the Platte watched as the Overland Mail became a highly organized enterprise under the direction of Ben Holladay.

Gilman's old friends assumed new roles along the Trail. Jerome Dauchy, who had been their partner the first year that they operated the Gilman ranch, had established a ranch of his own sixteen miles east of Alkali Springs. When the Pony Express terminated, Billy Campbell came to work for the Gilmans. Jacob Snell settled near Cottonwood Springs and the canyon near his ranch still bears his name.

Although the Nebraska City newspapers in the spring were filled with foreclosure sales, business on the Trail was good. Even mule trains, which generally started much later had started to Denver by February 8. By March 22, the ice on the Missouri River had broken up, and hordes of immigrants poured out on the docks all along the river.

Early in February, rumors of Indian attacks were carried by both travelers and the new telegraph line. Joseph P. Smith and his son-in-law, Mr. Anderson, had settled on Wood River. They, accompanied by three children, were cutting wood. Indians killed all five. Other incidents, however unrelated, caused people to think that the Confederacy was arming and inciting the Indians to attack those on the frontier. The *Nebraska City News* warned its readers on April 5 to watch out for "Jay Hawkers."

NEW STAGE SERVICE

Ben Holladay forced the sale of the Russell, Majors, and Waddell stage company for payment of money which they owed him. The line was advertised on December 31, 1861 over the objections of the owners. But they could not meet their payments, so in March 1862 the company was up for sale. Holladay offered $100,000. This was the highest bid for the company, their property, equipment and franchises.

In May as soon as the courts confirmed his title, Holladay hurried to survey the line. Practically all of the existing stations needed repairs, or to be replaced. New ones had to be built to provide a station every ten to fifteen miles. Quality horses and mules must be found and purchased. Of course his most demanding task was to find responsible men to replace those who had gone to war, or those questionable characters who cared little about the company's business. Men and material must be welded into a functioning organization if the enterprise were to succeed.

All summer Holladay's heavy freighting trains moved along the Trail carrying all kinds of supplies. Ben himself enjoyed the comforts of civilization and especially good food. This was the guiding principle as the new stations were established. Travel as described by Richard Burton in

1860 or by Horace Greeley in 1859 would be much different on the Holladay line.

Approximately every fifty miles comfortable home stations with dining rooms, hotel accommodations, and a telegraph office were built. These establishments with curtains at the windows and cloths on the tables were generally staffed with at least one woman.

Holladay did accomplish the organization which he desired. Each home station became a supply depot and a repair shop. Division agents moved constantly from station to station to keep everything in readiness for those all-important stage coaches.

Between the home stations, ranches, pony express stations or newly built stations provided for a stock tender and the agent. The small stage stations were made from logs, sod or in some places, stone. The floors were dirt. The walls were thick to make them secure from storms and from Indian attacks. It was a common sight to see a trench and a ridge dug around the station. This acted as a fire guard and could be used in fighting off attacks from Indians.

Crews of men were scattered along the Trail to build roads, improve bridges and even to survey better routes. The Holladay line must be the best transportation west of the Mississippi River.

Profits from his steamship lines and his mines were poured into the construction to realize his dream. The finest coaches in the country were made in Concord, New Hampshire. Not only strongly built, but their springs were tied to their strong axles and flexible thoroughbraces between the springs, making it possible for the coach to sway instead of transmitting all the bumps in the road to the passengers inside.

The coaches were not only sturdy and comfortable but attractive as well. The iron work was expecially crafted to follow the lines of the coach. The luggage boots, the window shades, and the well-padded upholstery were made of fine leather. There were inside and outside lamps. The bright red coaches, resting on yellow gear, were decorated with panels of western scenes painted by an English artist, John

Burgum. "Overland Stage" was lettered in gold. Light vehicles called "mud wagons" were used in very bad weather and in stretches where the Indians were a special threat.

Men sent out to buy horses and mules had a challenging task. Ben wanted only the best, and that led him into competition with the government which was buying horses for military service. Sometimes the buyers paid as high as $2000 for a single hitch of six blooded horses.

Ben set high standards for his drivers. He demanded no drinking on the job, courtesy to passengers and a minimum of profanity. These he enforced either personally or through his agents. But he added incentives for dependable drivers. He outfitted them as no others had ever been. Their corduroy suits were trimmed in black velvet. They were issued warm underwear, a caped coat, a wide brimmed hat and high leather boots and fine gloves. Each man was also given a silver-handled whip with a nine foot lash. Monthly pay of $100 made them aristocrats of the plains.

These splendid coaches and finely dressed drivers became the envy of the road. Pride and loyalty became part of the drivers, and many gave their lives to protect their responsibility.

Holladay carefully chose his agents. He kept the best of Russell, Majors, and Waddell's tough ones. Ben Ficklin, Nat Stein, and Jack Slade. He seemed to have an instinct for choosing others who feared only the Overland Boss. All were dedicated to one principle—the stages must go through regardless.

Gilman ranch became a swing station and Billy Campbell, the Pony Express rider, was hired to take care of the stock. A new station of cedar logs was built to the south and east of the ranch buildings.

The next four years, Holladay influenced all the activities from the Missouri River to Salt Lake City. One authority estimated that Ben spent $2,425,000 to equip the Overland. By 1864 he had forced every small line out of business, collected revenue from towns for stage line concessions, built toll bridges, hauled freight and express by his own freighting trains to new mines throughout the West. He possessed the greatest monopoly ever ruled by a single individual at that time. Records show at one time he employed 15,000 men, 20,000 wagons and 150,000 animals. But Ben would learn the hard lesson that governmental decisions would determine the destiny of transportation and of the "stage king" himself.

MEET MR. SMITH

One day when Jerry was heading for the corral, a horseman pulled up in front of the well. Jerry noticed his pale face and shaking hand. Was the man sick or drunk? The horseman introduced himself as John Smith. (This was a common name on the Trail, convenient if one were running away from the law or debts.) Jerry invited him to come in out of the hot sun and have a drink of cool water. After a few remarks, Smith told his story:

After I graduated at Yale College I thought that litera- ture was what I wanted to follow, and I tried my hand on a newspaper in Iowa, but finally determined to go west, and as everybody was striking out for Pike's Peak—it was "Pike's Peak or Bust"—I concluded to try Pike's Peak, and if I didn't like it, I would go through to Cali- fornia. I got to Omaha, and finally got in with a train; I had some horses, and I went along with the train, paying my bills for myself and my horses. I got right sick, and they thought I was going to die, I didn't know what I was about, thought so too; didn't much care what happened, and they left me at a ranch just down the road. I surprised them all by finally getting well but I have been sick a long time, lost everything, and I didn't get well very fast. There were Indians around all the time. I heard them talk, and sort of picked up the language. I have studied Latin and Greek and French, know something of other languages, and I found it wasn't difficult for me to pick up the Cheyenne language and the Sioux. I finally got well enough to ride a horse, but I don't have a cent left. Somebody got my horses, and I got cared for. Don't know exactly how it was arranged, but I was very much scared about myself. I am not getting my strength back very fast, and I am afraid to do anything much.

Smith was invited to spend a few days at the ranch. Long conversations about New England, tall stories of early days in New Hampshire and Connecticut were exchanged, much to the delight of Johnny McBride and the others around the ranch.

Good meals, cheerful company, and activity around the trading post helped Smith to regain his strength. He enjoyed practicing his Indian tongue with John Nelson and Two-Face when Two-Face came in for more supplies.

Nelson had learned that the Cheyenne were camped on Red Willow Creek, south of the loess bluffs. So John Gilman suggested that Smith might like to try his hand at trading with the Cheyenne. Two-Face would go with him to teach him the trade.

This arrangement proved very profitable to both parties. Every three or four weeks the two would return, bringing the best of the Cheyenne ware. By October, Smith had become enchanted with the Indian way of life. He agreed to be a trader for the Gilmans but would live with the Cheyenne. He rode off down the trail through the cedar canyon with a pack horse loaded with trading goods. Gilmans were not to see him for two years and then would hear a still stranger story about Mr. Smith from Yale.

In August, Colorado issued a charter for the new overland stage. Soon the daily red coaches with their beautiful horses and handsomely costumed drivers were dashing through the clouds of dust. Passengers—all kinds of passengers, even some from Europe—were transported by Mr. Holladay's luxury line. While some minor repairs were being made to harness or coach, tired, dusty travelers would often gather around the iron pump and drink from the common dipper.

One of the travelers who stopped was Samuel Clements, a young newspaper man. John Gilman's son wrote in 1932: "Among the noted men that stopped at our ranch was

Mark Twain when he crossed the plains to get material for his book *Roughin It*. For a long time my mother kept the chair he sat in at the table, but finally when they left there, in moving it was lost or broken."

THE PRAIRIE MOTOR

As colorful and as exciting as the stage coaches were, many dreamed of the day when railroads would finally come to the west. Until that time many inventive minds sought to improve transportation. Just such a man was General J. R. Brown. Now that a substantial road had been established west from Nebraska City, he built a steam engine that would pull a train replacing ox trains.

On Saturday, August 30, 1862, a long article appeared in the *Nebraska City News* describing this Prairie Motor, or steam wagon as it was later called. Plans were made for five regular stages leaving Nebraska City for Denver. The trip costing $75 would take one week by traveling day and night.

The engine arrived. Important people were invited to make a trial run, but a mile west of town this new wonder broke down. Brown located the difficulty but before he could order, and install the defective part, General Brown was called back to active duty. No one was courageous enough to continue his project. Six years later when Jerry Gilman looked out of the door of his new farmhouse back in Nebraska City he could see "Brown's folly," as it was called, rusting away under the hot Otoe County sun.

By September, settlers became alarmed about Indians. Settlers in Colorado called for the return of their troops from New Mexico. Indian trouble in Minnesota was serious.

But life was not all filled with fears and hardships. If there were one common trait among those hardy frontier men and women, it was their sense of humor. J. Sterling Morton was possibly the most important man in Nebraska City at this time. He was an editor, a farmer, a horticulturist, but chiefly a politician.

Many years later he described his adventure when he decided to go buffalo hunting out at Fort Kearny.

This excursion was in a wagon without springs; and after driving alone, as far as Weeping Water crossing, I overtook an ox train loaded with goods and supplies for Gilman's ranch on the Platte way beyond Fort Kearny.

One of the proprietors, Mr. Jed (Jerry) Gilman, was in command of the outfit, and by his cordial and hospitable invitation I became his willing and voracious guest for the noonday meal. With a township for a dining room over which arched the turquoise colored sky, like a vaulted ceiling, frescoed with clouds of fleece white, we sat down upon our buffalo robes to partake of a hearty meal. There was no white settler within miles of our camp. The cry of 'Dinner is now served in the next car' had never been heard west of the Mississippi River, nor even dreamed of in the East. The bill of fare was substantial: bacon, fried, hot bread, strong coffee, stronger raw onions, and roasted potatoes. And the appetite which made all exquisitely palatable and delicious descended to us out of the pure air and the exhilaration of perfect health. And then came the post prandial pipe —how fragrant and solacing its fumes—from Virginia natural leaf compared to which the exhalations from a perfecto cigar as today a disagreeable stench. There was then the leisure smile, the liberty and impulse to sing, to whoop and to generally simulate the savages into whose hunting grounds we were making an excursion. Life lengthened out before us like the Overland Route to the Pacific in undulations of continuously rising hillocks and from the summit of each one scaled we saw similarly attractive ones beyond in a seemingly never-ending pathway of pleasure, ambition and satisfaction.

But the smoke was over, the oxen again yoked to the wagons and the train, like a file of huge white beetles, lumbered along to the songs, swearing, and whip-cracking of the drivers toward the crossing of Salt Creek. However, by my persuasive insistence, Mr. Gilman left his wagon boss in charge and getting into my wagon accompanied me. Together we traveled briskly until quite late at night when we made camp at a point near where the town of Wahoo now stands. There was a rough ranch cabin there and we remained until the following morning when we struck out at a brisk trot toward Fort Kearny, entering the Platte valley at McCabe's ranch. The day and the road were perfect. We made good time. At night we were entertained at Warfield's on the Platte. The water in the well there was too highly flavored to be refreshing. Nine skunks had been lifted out of it the day of our arrival and only Platte river water could be had, which we found rather stale for having been hauled some distance in an old sorghum cask.

But fatigue and a square meal are an innocent opiate and we were soon fast asleep under the open sky with the moon and stars only to hear how loudly a big ranchman can snore in a bedroom of a million or more acres. In the morning of our third day out, we were up, breakfasted with the sunrise, and drove over the untried railroad bed of the Platte Valley at a rattling gait. The staunch and speedy animal over which the reins were drawn, a splendid bay of gentle birth had courage and endurance by heredity, and we made time.

Ranches were from twenty to thirty miles apart. And at night of the third day found us at Mabin's. This was a hotel, feed barn, dry goods establishment, and saloon all under one roof, about thirty miles from Fort Kearny. After a reasonably edible supper, Mr. Gilman and I were escorted to the saloon and informed that we could repose and possibly sleep in the aisle which divided it from the granary which was filled with oats.

Our blankets and buffalo robes were soon spread out in this narrow pathway. On our right were about two hundred bushels of oats in bulk, and on our left the counter which stood before variously shaped bottles containing alleged gin, supposed whiskey, and probably brandy. We had not been long in a recumbent position before—instead of sleep gently creeping over us—we experienced that we were race course and grazing grounds for innumerable myriads of sand fleas.

Immediately Gilman insisted that we should change our apartment and go out on the prairies near a haystack; but I stubbornly insisted that, as the fleas had not bitten me I would continue indoors. Thereupon Gilman incontinently left, and the fleas with vicious vigor and voracity assaulted me. The bites were sharp. They were incisive and decisive. They came in volleys. Then in wrath I too arose from that lowly but lively couch between the oats and the bar and sullenly went out under the starlit sky to find Mr. Gilman energetically whipping his shirt over a wagon wheel to disinfest it from fleas. But the sand fleas of the Platte are not easily discharged or diverted from fair and juicy victims. They have a wonderful tenacity of purpose. They trotted and hopped and skipped along behind us to the haystack. They affectionately and fervidly abided with us on the prairie; and it is safe to say that there never were two human beings more thoroughly perforated, more persistently punctured with flea bites than were the two guests at Mabin's ranch during all that long and agonizing night. However, there came an end to the darkness and the attempt to sleep, and after an early breakfast we resumed the Fort Kearny journey to arrive at its end in the late afternoon of the fourth day.

Martha, John Gilman's wife, had proved herself a true frontier lady. She had become accustomed to sod house living. She had added a woman's touch around the soddy where they lived. (While the store and some corrals were made from logs, many ranchers preferred to live in soddies because they were warmer in winter and cooler in summer.)

The Fitchie girls had been taught to be good housekeepers and cooks. Martha hung calico curtains at the tiny windows. Patchwork quilts topped the feather bed which covered the muslin ticks filled with prairie hay on the crude cedar bed in the corner. The iron stove was kept neatly blackened, and there were ironstone dishes on their scrubbed pine table.

On October 27, a tiny new rancher joined the Gilman household. Martha named the baby George. In 1932, shortly before his death, this same George wrote a letter to Mr. H. L. Williams of Gothenburg, Nebraska, stating:

"My mother told me that the cradle I used was made out of a bootbox, and on the end, printed in black letters, was 'French Calf.' The freighters going back and forth across the plains had many a good laugh about that cradle."

He also wrote: "The Indians used to come to the door and say to my mother, 'Ok-shee-la-took-tay?' (Where is the little boy? meaning me) and would take me to their tepees and keep me for hours at a time. The first suit I ever had was of buckskin, handsomely beaded, made by a Sioux squaw. I have it yet, and my son and grandson have had pictures taken in it." (According to George's daughter, this suit was given to the museum in San Diego, California.)

The year 1862 ended with still more rumors of Indian interference with the mail service. Between Fort Bridger and the Platte River, stock had been stolen, several men killed, and mailbags destroyed. But all was well at the Gilman ranch. There was money in the bank in Nebraska City, wood in piles for the winter and plenty of hay and provisions to last until spring.

Chapter VII
1863
NEW FORT NEAR THE PLATTE

The new year was ushered in by a message flashed along the telegraph line. President Lincoln issued the Emancipation Proclamation, freeing all the slaves in the states which were at war with the Union.

This was a gloomy spring for the North. Enlistments were down, so Congress resorted to a draft law which was so unpopular that riots erupted in several cities. Lincoln was still searching for a commander to lead the Union army. England and France were juggling with the idea of joining the South. And not until July after the battle of Gettysburg did the military situation improve for the Union.

All during 1862 and early 1863, the Sioux, Cheyenne and Arapahoe tribes were causing concern on the frontier. They were accumulating firearms and good horses. The stage stations were frequently raided, and Holladay's blooded horses fell into Indian hands. Dishonest white men, fugitives from the States, were doing a flourishing business supplying Indians with guns and "rot gut" whiskey. Reliable ranchmen refused to sell whiskey to the Indians, not only because the government prohibited it, but because Indians seemed to become instant alcoholics, unruly and dangerous. Territorial governors continued to plead for federal help in protecting the settlements and the roads. Ben Holladay even appealed to President Lincoln himself to provide troops to protect the stages and the stations.

Although Holladay appeared to be losing money in the stagecoach business, he found a new source of income. Pilgrims returning from the West told of men growing rich from the new mines near Virginia City, Nevada. Ben was able to secure some stock in the fabulous Ophir mine, and, placing the stock in his brother Jesse's name, he increased his assets. During this year also he added to his ships along the Pacific coast; and established trade with Maximilian in Mexico. Wells Fargo continued to grow rich and powerful in the West. Their success would, in three years, write a new chapter in the story of transportation, along all the routes across the country.

Life at the ranch was about as usual. There seemed never to be enough logs, hay or provisions to satisfy the customers. When the wagons left for Denver that year, they were accompanied by an outfit owned by Billy Campbell (Pony Boy) and his brother John. The Campbells took six wagons pulled by five pair of oxen to each wagon. The trains stayed close together and all the men were armed. The herders allowed the stock to graze as long as the evening light lasted, then herded them inside the corral made by the wagons. Sentries were posted lest the train be surprised by the unpredictable Indians.

At last the army heeded the call for soldiers to protect the Trail. Several units passed the ranch on their way to points near Salt Lake City. How welcome was the cool clear water from the iron pump. Many of the infantry had sore feet by the time they had marched from Fort Kearny to the ranch. Often they would make their camp near the ranch buildings and the officers would sometimes come over to the store to visit with those at the store and ask about the Indians, or tell of plans for getting free land under the Homestead Act after their service was over. (Daniel Freeman had filed the first claim on January 1, near Beatrice, Nebraska Territory.) But the news most welcome to the ranchers in this area was that there would soon be a new fort built in this vicinity.

It was on October 11 that Company F, Iowa Cavalry, under the command of Captain Nicholas J. O'Brien, stopped at the ranch to water and rest their horses. As was customary on the Trail, the newcomers were greeted and much information about the area exchanged. This was an occasion to be remembered, for the Gilmans entered into a friendly and profitable business association with Captain O'Brien and met for the first time a young soldier in the Quartermaster Corps by the name of Eugene Ware. Some time in the next few weeks, Company G. arrived, and Major George M. O'Brien, in command, became the commanding officer for the new Fort. (He was the older brother of Captain O'Brien.)

Many different stories have been told as to the reason for locating the new fort at the mouth of Cottonwood Canyon. Ware said it was because it was a great crossing for the Indians going north and south. The Indians had found it a good stopping place both winter and summer because of the fine grass and the scrubby willows and cottonwoods on the large island in the river at this point.

All the ranchers in the vicinity were employed to cut or haul cedars from the canyon. In a telegram to Major Easton on October 13, Major George M. O'Brien informed him that log barracks were being built for two companies of cavalry employing government transportation and soldiers doing the labor; but on October 20 he telegraphed that he was getting cedar logs from 12 to 15 miles from Cottonwood Springs but needed about 10,000 feet of lumber for partitions, flooring, doors and windows. He was directed to employ civilian carpenters on November 11. Ware said that Washington Hinman, William A. Anderson and John W. Lewis were employed.

This is what John Nelson had to say about the construction. "In the spring of 1863 (John was wrong about the season.) the government decided to build a fort at Cottonwood Springs, which was named and known as Fort McPherson.

"The Gilmans obtained the contract for building the fort. It was constructed of red cedar logs, of which I superintended the delivery. We had seventy men engaged in this work alone, besides several more who were chopping three hundred cords of wood for the use of the garrison, three companies of cavalry. We also secured the hay contract which kept us busy all summer.

"Besides other things, we did a tremendous trade in cedar wood, which parties returning to the states with empty wagons bought from us and sold for a handsome profit.

"In the autumn, business had increased to such an extent that the firm built another ranch at the Fort."

Several other ranchers found business very profitable with the coming of soldiers. McDonald rented his pilgrim quarters for the Post Headquarters until the regular one was built. O'Brien and Ware boarded with them until the officers' quarters were finished. Hinman found that blacksmithing was an important occupation with a cavalry post nearby. Pegleg Boyer, who kept a small store across the road stocked with canned goods and liquor, did a big business!

The new fort was officially named Cantonment McKean in honor of Brigadier-General Thomas McKean, then the commanding officer for the District of Nebraska. Local people called it Fort Cottonwood, and later, in 1866, it was officially renamed Fort McPherson.

Fortunately six of the soldiers were skilled wood-choppers. Other squads of men trimmed the branches, while still others used crosscut saws to cut the logs into the proper lengths. So the work was organized and much was accomplished each day.

The road ranchers removed their wagon boxes and extended the running gears to accommodate the twenty-foot logs. The best oxen were hitched to the wagons, and the logs were soon transported to a site which had been laid out about one mile west of the McDonald ranch buildings.

The best logs were saved for the headquarters building. These logs were "squared" by using the adz or were hewn with a broad ax. All the buildings had poled roofs interlaced with cedar boughs. Over the branches ten inches of hard clay was tamped to make a water and snow-proof

roof. Two whipsaws ripped the largest logs into lumber for the joists and bunks. The men covered the window openings with oiled paper to serve until window glass could be obtained.

Soon other buildings clustered about the parade ground. The 20' by 20' hospital was made of hewn logs located on the north side of the trail. A crude stable protected the horses from the winter wind. There was even a guardhouse complete with dungeon.

The proud day finally came when the flag flew from a flagstaff of its own, at the center of the parade ground, in front of the Headquarters Building, constructed from tall straight poles held together by iron joints fashioned by the blacksmith. This flagstaff rose above the valley's floor and became a beacon which welcomed travelers for the next seventeen years.

(Citizens of Lincoln County have erected a memorial shaft on this site, the only evidence of the once busy army post. In 1920 Mrs. Jerry Gilman came from her home in California to make a pilgrimage to this spot. She relived for a moment the days spent as a bride, in this wild country and to repeat again the story of how her husband had helped to erect this flagpole.)

The new troops were initiated into the life at the post by a windstorm on October 17. The straight wind filled with sand and gravel stampeded the horses and scattered tents and supplies over the prairie.

By Thanksgiving time the soldiers were reasonably comfortable. The Gilmans made several trips of the fifteen miles to help with the work and to share their knowledge of the country, of Indians and building skills needed on the prairie. They had offered, as had other ranchers, to furnish fat cattle for beef.

Preparations were being made at the ranch for Thanksgiving celebration. An invitation had been extended to Captain O'Brien and Eugene Ware to share in the festivities. All the men who could be spared from work, rode into the canyons to hunt wild game for the feast. Johnny McBride brought potatoes and onions from the root cellar,

Monument marking the site of the Fort McPherson flagpole

a pit which had been carefully dug in the ground and lined with hay. When Jerry had brought the supplies in October a quantity of potatoes, onions, turnips and cabbage were placed in the pit and covered with sand and a layer of sod. This protected the vegetables from freezing. Several dozen eggs had been buried in fine salt to keep them from freezing and to insure their freshness. These were kept in a keg in the house.

For several days before the big occasion the odors of baking bread, roasting meat and of course apple pie came from Martha's sod house.

Martha covered a large "improvised" table in the store with her two red-and-white-checked tablecloths. Everyone from soldiers to herders shared the quantity of food prepared by Martha and Frenchie, the cook. Little George toddled about, bounced on knees, and stuffed his mouth with food. It was the first time that some of the men had eaten "off a tablecloth" for a long time.

Conversation at the table matched the good food. John Gilman was at his best with good food, a pipe filled with fragrant tobacco and an appreciative audience. He told about their home in New Hampshire. Every story was told with the emphasis on the humorous side. Jerry added comments and details to John's stories.

Jerry told how John hated to plow the rocky old New Hampshire soil in early summer, so he slipped away and hired out, guiding climbers up dangerous Mount Washington in New Hampshire although he had not been trained as a mountain climber!

John described the time he had convinced government men that he was well acquainted with engineering and the sea. He was hired and sent on his way to New Orleans to help improve the port there, but he did not stay long in the South. Having a chance to hitch a ride on a freighter loaded with lumber, he headed for Boston. The ship, which was old and unseaworthy, was shipwrecked in the Gulf of Mexico, and John was almost drowned. However, he and some others floated on a raft for several days, surviving on flour that had been spilled on the raft. (Eugene Ware related a more dramatic version of this story.)

The conversation turned to more serious things. O'Brien evidently impressed by the characters of these two men, asked how they came to be out here in this lone ranch, for they appeared to be men who could hold their own in the most civilized society.

John explained how the wagon broke down on their way to Denver. (They had dreams of eventually going on to California.) He described their trade with the Indians, demonstrating that now they could speak both Sioux and Cheyenne, and repeated the stories of John Smith and John Nelson, who lived part time with bands of Indians and were able to trade so well.

Jerry, laughingly, explained that Indians gave every white man a name. They had named him Po-te-sha-sha, which meant "red whiskers." John was labeled We-Chox-Cha, meaning "the old man with a pump." Their business really had grown because of the trade in oxen. They had started with their own teams, trading one good ox for two footsore trail animals, or by selling the animal for a good price. The footsore cattle were turned out on the fine pasture north of the ranch and in a short time were ready for trade. (About 200 head of cattle were kept over the winter.) John took O'Brien into the back room and showed him barrels, kegs and sacks of supplies which they kept on hand for trade or sale.

The men went out to the hay stacks which encircled the corral, and when O'Brien saw the quality of hay he suggested that they not sell all of their hay so the fort might have a supply if they needed it in the spring. An arrangement was also made for the delivery of good beef to the fort if the district quartermaster's approval was granted.

While O'Brien and the Gilmans discussed business, others around the ranch were entertaining themselves by racing horses in the open prairie south the ranch buildings. Although by Thanksgiving time, travel on the trail had dwindled to a few supply trains and the

108

stagecoaches, there were many men who stayed at the ranch at least part of the winter. Some herded, some cut wood, others trapped animals—muskrats to brown bear. Almost as popular as buffalo skins were the pelts from the big buffalo or prairie wolves.

On December 18, Captain Bradshaw of the Quartermaster's Corps sent the freighting train that brought the needed stoves, supplies, doors and sashes that the infant military post so desperately needed. According to a telegram sent to headquarters by O'Brien, they still needed lumber for bunks in the hospital.

As given before, John Nelson stated that business was so good at Gilmans that the firm built a second ranche (ranch) at the fort. Family references were often made to the store which the brothers had at the fort. The attempt to locate this ranch site has been in vain. Since they kept stock there, it had to be far enough from McDonalds to be profitable. Sam Fitchie, Martha's brother, lived near Box Elder Canyon. There was a stage station in this vicinity. One clue is given when Colonel S. W. Summers, then in charge of the Fort, sent a telegram to Lieutenant F. A. McDonald which said:

"One Fitchie and a hired man of Gilmans' claim possession of 1/2 mile front and one mile running north taking in island which lies north of the south channel upon which we are cutting wood. Fitchie asks that we cease cutting wood and that the wood shall not be removed. They have a fence on the south end and the two sides are fenced to the channel. I desire instructions." signed Col. Summers.

Sam Fitchie wrote years later that he, his sister and her little boy were surrounded by 300 Indians, barely escaping with their lives. It is reasonable to assume that the store or ranch was near the military reservation near the Fitchie ranch. It is also reasonable to assume that more than excess profits were involved. Knowing John Gilman's desire to be where the action was, it is logical that he would want to be near the Fort, the telegraph office, and other merchants at Cottonwood Springs; also with a woman and child in the home, neighbors and a doctor were important.

At the year's end the stagecoaches were traveling at irregular intervals. Two or three coaches traveled together, with drivers, guards and even passengers heavily armed. All coaches carried mail, and occasionally a mail wagon accompanied the coaches. John Nelson commented upon his activity at the last of the year:

"I was sent out trading again, and this time my pay was five dollars a day or one hundred and fifty dollars a month. I had two waggons, each drawn by six yoke of oxen, and two men to assist me. We went to the Republican River, and there found a band of Cheyenne.

"We drove into their camp, not knowing who they were until we got right amongst them. They refused to let us leave, and soldiered us, that is, placed sentries all around the outfit. Their object was to force us to trade with them at their price, a fourth below ours. This I refused to do. Then they became very angry, and declined to trade at all or permit me to leave the camp.

"After a week I succeeded in bringing them round to my view of things, and commenced to trade. When a few robes had changed hands they tried to do me again and recommenced their old tactics. Finally I "squared" White Antelope, the chief, by giving him a feast of apples baked with rice and served with hot coffee. This had the desired effect, and we traded off pretty satisfactorily.

"However, the business was not nearly so remunerative as my previous venture had been, and I determined not to trouble the Cheyennes again for their custom."

Business in 1864 would be still less profitable as the Indians continued to resent the slaughter of the bison, the miles of emigrant wagons, the presence of soldiers on their hunting ground.

Chapter VIII

1864
TIDES OF FIRE!

The red iron pump on the prairie continued to dispense cold, clear water even during the subzero weather, but travelers on the Trail seemed more interested in hot coffee which simmered in the huge coffeepot on the back of the stove in the store. Chilled passengers from the stagecoaches or travelers on horseback frequently came to the store to purchase food or whiskey. Whiskey was a popular commodity on the trail. There were those who believed that whiskey would cure all kinds of ills, even snakebite. Prohibition had not reached this part of the country.

Good whiskey was expensive at Gilmans. Most of it came from the distilleries located in the east, some even was imported from Scotland. Regular customers soon learned to expect the real product at this trading post. Many unscrupulous traders, however, found a profitable substitute for the expensive brands. They would buy a barrel of pure alcohol, mix it with a barrel of water, some plug tobacco and a sprinkling of red pepper. At even ten cents a drink, this gave a huge profit. This was called "Pilgrim Whiskey," Rot Gut, or Red Eye. It even found its way into Indian camps, much to the distress of the intelligent Sioux chiefs. It was generally accepted that all ranchers, freighters and traders drank hard liquor. Many young men did sign Majors' pledge in good faith. Jerry

Gilman did not like "spirits," so his colds, snakebites and other excuses were not doctored from the flat bottle.

The bitter January weather did not entirely discourage travelers. During January and February at least twenty coaches of Mormon officers or missionaries went past, going or coming. They no longer held to the trail north of the river but crossed over and moved along the well-worn Oregon-California Trail. They had no fear of the Indians and seemed to move freely, not accepting military escort nor joining other trains of armed stagecoaches.

One morning in January the sky seemed filled with gray mist. It felt as though a warm spring rain would descend at any time, but instead about one o'clock in the afternoon, small icy flakes of snow began to fall. Suddenly a cold north wind swept over the river, and the plains became a giant grinder of whirling, cutting ice. Men and beasts were encased in frozen cotton.

Fortunately, the loggers had stayed at the ranch that day to stack the wood, grease the wagons, and shoe the oxen. But a mule train coming from Leavenworth loaded with shelled corn and flour for Denver was not so fortunate. It had left the camping ground near the Gilman ranch headquarters in the morning and had traveled some ten or twelve miles west when the wind struck. When the train was trapped in the white gusts, the wind literally blew the animals away.

After the storm had cleared one could see overturned wagons, broken tongues, and tattered canvas, corn and flour scattered everywhere. By some miracle, the men escaped injury.

In a day or two a forlorn train of empty wagons pulled by animals saved or recaptured from the storm passed the ranch on their way back to Leavenworth. Men with frostbitten hands salvaged a few sacks of grain and flour and stored them at the fort.

Bad weather continued for several weeks, but the hired men made occasional trips across the valley to the canyon to bring back more cedars. One day George Laird, who had been working at the ranch for some time, got the bright idea of poisoning skunks up in the canyons, in order to save precious ammunition. They prepared a can of meat fryings and arsenic and fastened it to the last wagon. When they arrived at the wood site, the grease was gone. All that effort seemed in vain. The can had disappeared somewhere along the trail. When they returned to the ranch in the evening, imagine their surprise to see at the mouth of the canyon, a dead Indian with the can of grease at his side.

It was customary for the Indians to gather near Laramie in the spring to receive the tribute which the government distributed to them for the use of the road through their territory as prescribed by treaty. Not only did the Indians receive supplies, but they also traded among themselves. John Nelson, Gilman's trader, saw an opportunity to trade for some quality buckskins. So he took a wagon of trading goods and a helper up the Trail to Laramie.

By March a few mule trains were on the Trail. It was good to visit with the freighters. The newspapers stated that President Lincoln had given supreme command to tough old Ulysses S. Grant. Veterans who had known Grant vowed that he would soon end the war.

A GUN AND A ROPE

But other news came from the west, not gossip this time. Captain Slade had kept his promise, to free his division of the Holladay Stage Company of outlaws and to keep the Indians under control. But by 1862 his drunken sprees caused people in Denver and along the Trail to fear the "boss" more than the outlaws. When Slade and his gang wrecked the sutler's store at Fort Halleck, the sutler sent a telegram to Ben Holladay, and Holladay fired Slade.

Slade became a freighter, hauling goods between Fort Bridger and Salt Lake City. When prospectors found gold in Alder's Gulch up in Montana, Slade bought a ranch in Montana. He continued to trade and haul supplies. He called his new home Spring Dale. It was near Virginia City.

A Vigilante group was formed to control the lawlessness around the mining area. Some say that Slade himself became a member. But he soon tired of the orderly life. Throughout the winter, his escapades increased in number and viciousness. His favorite sport, when he was drunk, was to ride into a saloon and shoot out the lights, or order a drink for his horse. Many insisted that he would toss Jules Beni's ears on the counter in payment for a drink.

On March 10, 1864, Jack Slade invaded Virginia City. He wrecked about every establishment in town. The Vigilante Committee met, held court, and sentenced Joseph A. Slade to hang by the neck until he was dead.

One of his friends rode out to tell his wife, and she rode as fast as she could, but was too late to save his life. Many conflicting stories are told about Virginia Dale Slade. Some say that she was a beautiful woman who attracted everyone who saw her. Others say that she was another big-boned, rough frontier woman. But all the story tellers agreed that she could ride a horse with the best of them, and could handle a gun almost as well as her husband.

Virginia vowed that Slade would not be buried in Montana, so she had him sealed in a tin coffin filled with whiskey. When the stage road was opened in the spring to Salt Lake City, she took him there for burial.

When those at the Gilman ranch heard this bit of news, they shook their heads and wondered how a man with so much ability could cause so much sorrow and end up in an unmarked grave.

*   *   *

April not only brought spring weather and swarms of all kinds of vehicles on the Trail, but the wives and relatives of the settlers around Fort Cottonwood. Many of them had "wintered" in Nebraska City or Omaha. There was something about the brass howitzers and the cavalry that inspired confidence. McDonald, the rancher at Cottonwood Springs, planned a dance. Ranchers and farmers and about twenty of their womenfolk came by wagon or buggy, or on horseback, riding or walking as far as twenty-five miles.

John Gilman proudly swung his pretty, dark-haired wife to the tunes of "Turkey in the Straw" and "Soap Suds over the Fence."

PUFFS ON A PEACE PIPE

In early April Captain Logan of the First Colorado Cavalry came down the Trail from Denver, stopping at each ranch and farm along the way. He warned of the possibility of an Indian war, and tried to ascertain the provisions for defense at each settlement. So the ranchers were not surprised when on April 16, 1864, General Mitchell and Lieutenant Williams arrived at Fort Cottonwood to hold council with the head men of the Sioux. General Logan had believed that if the Sioux could be "won over" it would be simpler to handle the Cheyenne and the others.

Precautions were taken at the ranch to see that all the guns and ammunition were ready in case of trouble, as the tribes began to assemble two miles outside of the fort. Herders were urged to keep the stock within range of the ranch site until after the council had adjourned. The council lasted all day, with many speeches, and the only gain was an agreement to meet again in fifty days. General Mitchell promised to stop the survey parties in the Niobrara area and to ask permission to make a new treaty.

The Indians were fed, and the chiefs in turn invited a delegation of the officers to a dog feast. This was a Sioux delicacy, a stew prepared from fattened puppies. An important chief at this council was Spotted Tail, who would participate in future councils.

The Indians seemed to vanish during the night and the settlers turned their attention to the affairs around the ranches and the hundreds of pilgrims moving along the Trail. Since the dance at McDonalds had been so successful, another was planned late in April when the Eleventh Ohio Cavalry stopped on their way west. No royal ball was more exciting. Officers in their best dress uniforms, passengers from the stage including several women, some girls who had come to the Cottonwood

Springs vicinity to settle or to work, attended the dance along with the neighboring ranchers. The night was clear and the sky was filled with a million stars. Outside one could smell the wild plum blossoms. The sounds of laughter and skeins of fiddle music pushed fear far away beyond the rim of the canyons. Jerry Gilman wished for pretty, auburn-haired Elizabeth Fitchie, Martha's little sister, back at Nebraska City.

Ben Holladay made one of his flying trips across the country. The stage agents learned that he had received a new mail contract to deliver mail 450 miles north of Salt Lake City. He added 29 new shiny coaches to his fleet of four wheelers. Towns were now paying tribute to Holladay for a stage making regular trips to their settlements. Denver and Holladay continued to feud over mail and stage services. The Denver newspaper blasted him as being the most hated man in the west.

With more wagons traveling westward than ever before, with no organized police force or courts, justice was often left to the next army post. According to Eugene Ware, even the Gilman ranch became a court of law.

On May 7, Captain O'Brien, the commanding officer at Fort Cottonwood, had ridden down to the Gilman ranch to make arrangements for cutting a large quantity of hay during the summer. While he was there, the Ingram and Christie (a well known freighting company) wagon train stopped in front of the store, and a sergeant came looking for the captain. He reported that a Mr. Trivit of Denver had stopped at the Fort and entered a complaint against the train owners, saying that they had defrauded him of a large amount of money. Two members of the train were put under arrest at the Fort and were sent down to Gilmans. The captain tried the case and sent the culprits on their way.

SMOKE SIGNALS

Stories concerning the Indian depredations continued all along the Trail. But the dangers were becoming very real. One day a lone wagon north of the river across from Fort Cottonwood was attacked in daylight, the wagon burned, men killed and the horses stolen, but the soldiers who saw the attack were unable to go to the rescue because the Platte was flooding. Gilmans' men working in the canyon cutting cedars had seen about twenty Cheyenne appear on the bluffs near the canyon.

Since Gilmans had contracts to cut hay, furnish beef, and to cut logs for a new fort farther west (Fort Sedgwick) John decided that the government should make some effort to protect the Gilman ranch. He rode up to the Fort, this time putting his request in writing. But O'Brien, already faced with too many problems, denied John's request, suggesting if he wanted protection he should come to the fort. John replied angrily, "I will hold the United States government responsible if I lose stock or property for want of protection."

As soon as John got back to the ranch he rounded up the help and directed them: "Drop whatever you are doing and let's start fortifying on our own. The logs piled over there are part of the Sedgwick contract. If they can wait to furnish us protection, we can wait to furnish logs."

A trench three feet deep was dug around the store, the well, and the sod houses. The poles which had been cut were twelve feet long. These were set on end and held together by braces placed on the inside. A gate was hung on the north side facing the Trail. The stage station and the corrals were scattered too far apart to be encompassed within the cedar palisade.

Threats of Indian attacks increased the work at the ranch. Wagon trains stored possessions or supplies, planning to call for them later. Many travelers were spending several days or weeks before venturing out on the open Trail again. Small trains waited to join larger ones for safety.

But not all the boarders were afraid of the Indians. One day an odd-looking little wagon pulled by a team of horses stopped. The driver asked for a drink of water. The wagon was equipped with cloth, buttons, and other tools of a tailor's trade. The itinerant called himself Farley. He was low on cash so he made a deal with the brothers. He offered to make them suits for the price of the material alone if they would allow him and his horses to stay at the ranch. He was a master story teller so he was a welcome guest. He accompanied Jerry up to the fort with samples of blue cloth suitable for uniforms. He was able to make a profit tailoring uniforms for the officers before he moved on with another large train going to Denver.

MR. SMITH RETURNS

Sam Fitchie, who had been trapping around the army post as well as caring for Gilmans' small beef herd near Box Elder Canyon, came down to the outer ranch. He had news.

Two days before, a man wearing ragged buckskin breeches had stumbled into the Fort. He was sunburned, muddy, and scratched. He seemed dazed. Soldiers gathered around. He was nearly incoherent, but did manage to say his name was John Smith. With the number of John Smiths on the Trail, Eugene Ware was not impressed. This man looked as though he had been a perennial bum, so Ware suggested that he move on and get out of camp as soon as possible.

Sam Fitchie was not quite so dubious. He did slightly resemble the John Smith who had worked for the Gilmans a couple of years ago. Sam helped him on the back of his saddle and took him to his soddy. After a shave, a good hot bath, some clean clothes and a good night's sleep, Smith told his story:

After leaving the Gilmans to live with the Cheyenne, I married the daughter of the chief of the band there on Red Willow. He wasn't the head of the Cheyennes, but he was the head of that band. And I got a nice tepee

118

(tent) and some horses and dogs and two children, one of them a boy and the oldest a girl, and I was considered one of the band. When there was anything to come up, they asked me what I thought about it, and I never tried to become chief or anything of that kind, and consequently I didn't have any trouble with any ambitious Indian. I was living there all right until they tried to get the Cheyenne into this war. I saw there was going to be a whole lot of trouble.

Indians from the south came up there, and things got distracted. They called a large meeting down near the mouth of Red Willow where our camp then was and there came in Cheyenne from down below. The meeting was a big meeting. We had a big bonfire, and the young bucks were all talking war, and I didn't know exactly what to do. My wife told me that there was going to be trouble, and if I wasn't careful some of them would shoot me. One evening at a big campfire there was an Indian who said he was a Kioway, I don't know whether he was or not. He was an Indian that spoke a different dialect from any that I knew of, but he could talk Cheyenne as plain as anybody, and he talked long and loud.

He had set up a post near the fire, like a fence post, and he had put a soldier's hat on it, that had the brass cross-sabers and trimmings of a cavalry soldier's hat. He would talk and get excited and with his tomahawk he would chop into this hat on the post. I tilted up the corner of the tent and listened to all of it and my wife went out to listen better. I saw the uproar getting greater and greater, and some of the young bucks got excited, and went shooting their guns into the air. My wife went and got a pony as if leading it out to grass, and took it outside of camp up in the brush, and put a saddle and bridle on it, and told me where to find it. Then she told me to slip out and get on it and skip, while she went and sat down near the scene and watched what was going on. I thought things might cool down, but the spasm grew worse, and they got to howling and yelling, and singing war songs, and everybody was around the campfire.

I kissed my two children good-bye, little half breeds, but mighty pretty for Indians; I slid out, and got on the horse and rode. I struck for Cottonwood Canyon. It is a pretty long trip, but I rode pretty fast, and I got to the headbreaks about dawn, when right out of the grass in front of me rose two Cheyenne Indians, both of them with bows and arrows, and I didn't have a gun. I was a refugee. I didn't dare have a gun. They took me prisoner. I said to myself, 'Now my time has come.'

They asked me where I was going, and I told them that I was going down to Cottonwood Canyon to get some ammunition and supplies and whiskey. My pony was plumb used up, and they made me get off, and one of them said, 'Come with us.'

I said, 'No, I wanted to go down and get my stuff. Then the Cheyenne drew an arrow up to its head, and punched it up against me, and of course, knew if he let go of the bow string the arrow would go right through me. I supposed they would take me down to the canyon, tie me to a tree, build a fire around me, and have some fun. I had to go but kept thinking, and watching for something to do in the way of escape, when all at once they stopped and one of them went into some bushes and pulled out a little keg of Indian whiskey. Then I saw that both had been drinking, and that their actions were due to drink. The whiskey was awful stuff, made out of alcohol, water, red pepper, and molasses, and these two Indians had got this keg hidden up in the breaks at the head of Cottonwood Canyon, and were having a great time. One of them had a big tin cup and he filled it plum full, and handed it to me to drink. I said to him it would kill me, that I couldn't drink it. And they told me that I must drink it, and I took a sip. Then they told me to go on drinking; then they would draw arrows each one up to its head with the bow thus drawn punch me in the sharp point of the arrow. They would punch me in the ribs with it, they would punch me in the neck with it. I knew if they would relax just a little and the arrow was released I was a dead man. I said to myself, they are going to get me drunk and then roast me. I would take a sip and they would laugh in a diabolical manner, and draw the arrow up again to the full, and punch me with it and say, 'Drink.'

Well, I kept sipping and expostulating, but it

wouldn't do. I concluded I would rather be roasted drunk than sober. One of them would laugh and howl as he watched the other one punch me with drawn arrow, and they would take turns at this, and take turns laughing. Well, I don't know, but I guess I drank it all up. I bade myself goodbye, and farewell, and did it more than once. I know I kept sipping and they kept prodding me with drawn arrows. I remember falling to the ground, and trying to get up, and I remember those fellows dancing around, shouting and having fun, while I was thinking my end had come.

Well, sir, I wasn't hurt. I woke up with hardly any clothes on. They took my moccasins and my coat. When I woke up the sun was shining down on me, hot and blistering, and I didn't know where I was. I didn't know whether I was dead or alive, and such raging thirst and fever I never had. My head was bursting wide open, my mouth all dry and crisp. My tongue was rough like sharkskin. I tried to get up, but fell over, and it sort of began to dawn on me that I was alive. There was nobody around, and I couldn't tell where I was. I finally saw the depressions on the ground, and I made up my mind that I must find water. I went stumbling down grade and every once in a while I would fall over, and lie there. After a while I would get up and I thought I would choke to death, and never find water.

From time to time I went down and would fall, and have a momentary lapse of memory. Finally I struck a little muddy pool, and I went into it, drank and vomited; drank and rolled over in the water and mud and lay there.

Finally I struck a place where I just lay down in the water and went to sleep. I kept waking up; and that is the way I went down to Cottonwood Canyon.

Now in fact, I wasn't in the danger I thought I was in. These Cheyenne had been out on an expedition to get some whiskey, and didn't know what was going on in the village. I thought they had been sent out to intercept me, but as a matter of fact they didn't know anything about what was going on. They were having some private fun with me. That was an Indian way of having fun. But I never expected to get through without being tied to a tree and burned . . . I would like to see those two children, and have no doubt that I will. My Indian wife is all right, first class for an Indian, but I got about through my wanting to live the life of an Indian.

Sam Fitchie chuckled and said, "When the soldiers saw John Smith all cleaned up they hired him and another character we call Hunter to bring in buffalo, deer meat or wild turkey and they will pay them by the pound.

STORM CLOUDS

Fears of an Indian uprising multiplied. The Gilmans hired men to cut hay in the bottoms, carrying guns with them on the mowing machines. Part of the crews cutting cedars in the canyons took turns watching while others cut.

About May 21, Joe Jewett and John Sharp, old hunters and stage drivers stopped on their way to the fort. They said Cheyenne and Brule bucks had surrounded a detachment of Colorado soldiers on Turkey Creek southwest of Fort Kearny.

About that time, Two-Face returned from trading with the Brule Sioux north of the river. He told the Gilmans that a Cheyenne chief had been up through the bands showing a sergeant's cavalry jacket, a watch and other souvenirs. He was encouraging the Brules to war dance, and Two-Face warned that the Brules might attack.

Smoke signals and fire arrows, at night, were seen all up and down the valley. Smith and Hunter went down to Red Willow to contact the Cheyenne for information but found them hostile.

Soon the east bound stagecoaches were loaded with frightened women and children from the ranches and farms who were hurrying to Fort Kearny for safety. John had been up to Cottonwood Springs and stopped at McDonalds. Mrs. McDonald and the laundress, Linty, were the only women left there. When John returned they discussed whether Mat and Little George should go also, but Mat decided to take her chances inside the cedar palisade rather than on the road in a coach.

Word came through on June 11 that Denver was in a state of panic. Hungate, his wife, and two children had been killed at their ranch just three miles from Denver. Cheyenne were attacking pilgrims on the Smoky Hill road, along the Arkansas River as well.

On July 19, General Mitchell came again to try to hold a council with the Sioux, bringing a battalion of Pawnee Indian soldiers under the command of Captain North of Columbus, N.T. The council solved nothing and almost ended in a fight between the Sioux and their old enemy, the Pawnee.

General Mitchell and other army officers who had been in the west for some time, were sincere in trying to work out a solution for the many problems. But other officers fresh from the battles of the Civil War in the east believed that "Only a dead Indian is a good Indian." They issued commands to "Kill the squaws and papooses. You kill the nits to destroy the lice." All the fine treaty promises made to the Indians by conscientious army officers were disregarded or broken. These new officers made no attempt to sort out the hostiles from the friendlies.

On the other hand, there were sober, wise Indian chiefs who recognized that the White Man was here to stay and that fighting would not solve the problems. Spotted Tail took his band to the Bighorn Mountains away from the Trail. O-Way-See-Cha, chief of the Ogalla Sioux, had meant to keep his promise to General Mitchell but he was unable to control his hot-headed young warriors from raiding.

The presence of renegade white men who posed as Indians added to the problem. They not only sold guns and whiskey to the Indians but actually attacked wagon trains for plunder.

When Jerry went to Nebraska City for supplies, he met his old friend, Herman Angell. Herman was still making and repairing shoes. Herman accepted Jerry's invitation to come to the ranch.

In August, Mat's sister, Mary Jane Fitchie, was to come for a visit. She was nineteen years old, taller than Mat but with the same sparkling black eyes. Even though the stages might be traveling in caravan, Mat could not help worrying about her sister's safety. Finally on August 8, she arrived, tired out by the rough ride over 'washboard' roads.

Although the story of the attack has already been told, it is interesting to hear Billy Campbell's version which was repeated again and again. In an interview many years later he said:

"She was at breakfast with the family when a band of Indians rode up. No one thought anything of this because John Gilman often employed Indians, and fed and entertained them. But suddenly there came shots and a stampede, and the Indians ran off the Gilman stock, killing the three men who were tending it. (The three men killed were not the herders.)

"John Gilman had to act fast. There were some horses in the barn that the Indians had overlooked. (These could have been stage horses, since Holladay did not file a claim for stock.) These were hitched up swiftly to a wagon. The three dead men were thrown across the floor in front of the driver's seat, where they wouldn't roll around. Jennie climbed beside the driver. John Gilman dropped the family silver into her lap; 'Jennie, take care of this!' The three widows, one with an infant, rode behind her in the wagon, and the nineteen-year-old girl, with her feet on the corpses, and one hand holding the Gilman belongings, turned and used the other hand to comfort the weeping women. Jennie's sister rode in a carriage, (probably a buggy) while John and only two men formed the guard. They drove at a wild speed to McPherson, seventeen miles off. They were not molested, which seemed funny because they heard Indians all around them and occasionally caught sight of a bobbing head feather. Later John Gilman heard the reason. Old Two-Face, an Indian who had often worked for him before the uprising, told him:

" 'Minnehaska' (the name Indians have called white men since the days of the colonies; it means long knife) 'we saw you and your women and we followed you to keep other braves from killing you. You fed me, paid me. You, my friend. I, your friend.' "

Meanwhile back at the ranch, Jerry, Herman Angell, and the stage agent had stayed to protect, if they could, the ranch buildings. They set about trying to prepare themselves for an expected attack.

The stage company had left two supply wagons which should be unloaded and the grain stored, but the men decided to stay within the palisade and leave the wagons unprotected. They loaded all the guns that they had in the store, and placed them about the palisade. They pumped buckets of water, in case of fire. Then waited. The heat, the silence, and the flies tortured the three.

Finally, Jerry climbed up on the roof, carrying his gun and spy glass. He could scarcely believe what he saw. Literally hundreds of war-painted Sioux on ponies had evidently crossed the Platte River, a half-mile to the north of the ranch and were riding full speed over the prairie surrounding the ranch buildings that would burn like tinder. Only an army could head them off.

By this time the other men had heard the yells. Angell joined Jerry on the roof. Here they stood.

Almost immediately, the Indians set fire to the supply wagons. Jerry made a quick decision. He saw that this was a Sioux war party. Better die from an arrow than to be burned alive. Throwing down his gun, he shouted, "Cola, cola!" Recognizing one of the bucks, he called his Indian name. The young Indian stopped and turned. Jerry began to address him in Sioux language. John Nelson, John Smith and Two-Face had been good teachers. Jerry spoke like a blood brother.

The young brave held up his hand, and said, "Cola, Minnehaska!" He turned and shouted to the others and then started riding east as fast as his horse could run. The rest of the band followed. Only the burning freight wagons were left behind to remind the whites of their narrow escapes. (In later years, when Jerry would retell this experience to his family, he always remarked that it was because he had an Angell beside him that his life was spared.)

Billy Campbell and his brother, John, had got as far as the camping ground near Jack Morrow's ranch on their way back from Denver. They could see an unusual amount of activity around the stage station near the ranch. When Billy rode up he was told about the Indian attacks and the massacre at Plum Creek. (Eleven men were killed and Mrs. Morton and a boy named Dannie Marble were captured.) "You had better get John and move up here quickly, Billy, because there are redskins all around.

"Everybody was glancing feverishly right and left at every little patch of sage, and I wheeled and raced for John. Half a mile was no ride for a Pony Express boy, but I guess I never carried the mail as fast as I carried that bad news to my brother. We hitched up in a rush, and made a run for the station, expecting every foot of the way that a painted Sioux would jump out and finish us.

"From Jack Morrow's we all rode double file into Fort McPherson, for the word had gone out to all settlers to congregate at the army posts as it became known that the uprising was general. We rode down the middle of the valley, away from the bluffs and rises that afforded ambush spots. The best we could muster were a few old shotguns and squirrel rifles, and one Winchester would have been better than the lot. However, we reached McPherson in safety. That was like an old home to me. More so than ever this time, for I had no sooner ridden in than I saw for the first time a girl so pretty that I fell in love with her at once. She was a shapely lass of nineteen, with the stride and the way about her that bespoke an outdoor girl. On all sides of me I heard the men exclaiming over her, and it was not because the sight of a white woman was rare to them in McPherson. There were many others but no other like her. Officers, men, civilians—everyone paid attentions to her and called her the belle of the prairies. She had jet-black hair and black eyes that snapped at you even when they were filled with the horror that she had just been through.

"I got acquainted with her as quick as I could, and she

told me about herself. Her name was Mary Jane Fitchie. She was called Jennie, and lived with her family on a farm near Nebraska City. She told me that she had come west to visit her sister, Mrs. John Gilman.

"In the days that followed there were dances and other gayeties but John Gilman was as vigilant a chaperon as a Spanish duenna. He had ideas as to whom a young girl should associate with, and his sister-in-law was carefully shielded from contact with the rough frontier characters."

INDIAN WAR OF '64

While those living along the Trail had been warned that Indians were liable to attack, no one was quite prepared for the simultaneous attacks upon the stations between Julesburg and into the valley of the Little Blue.

George H. Carlyle, Ben Holladay's master of transportation, describes this scene in an affidavit sworn to before Probate Judge John C. Liddell, and submitted to a Senate investigating committee on Ben Holladay's losses:

"August 9, 1864 I left Alkali Station for Fort Kearny, on reaching Cottonwood Springs I learned by telegraph that the Indians had attacked a train of 11 wagons at Plum Creek, killed 11 men, captured one woman, burned the wagons and run off stock. Upon hearing this I started down the road and when within a few hundred yards of Gilman Station, met a large body of Indians who had just killed Gillette and two other men, a short distance east of Gilman's Station, and had run off Gilman's and Dan Smith's stock; these Indians followed the coach nearly 20 miles, waiting for a chance to attack it. I saw the bodies of Gillette and two men lying on the ground, they were fearfully mutilated and full of arrows. At Plum Creek I saw the bodies of 11 men that the savages had murdered and I helped to bury them.

"I also saw the fragments of the wagons still burning. I also saw the dead body of the man that was killed by the Indians at Smith's and the ruins of the ranch which had been burned.

"On reaching Kearny, I turned back to Cottonwood. On my way up, saw seven Indians at Midway Station from which station the Indians had driven the employees of the line; these Indians, seeing the coach coming up, ran off into the hills; on going into the house, found they had destroyed all the dishes, furniture, etc. I then moved the stage horses to Dan Smith's and Miller and Peniston's ranch at which place the settlers had flocked for mutual protection against the savages.

"On returning down the road I found the Indians had visited Platte Station and had stolen four stage horses. I continued going backwards and forward over the route until about the 16th of August when orders were given by Mr. Otis, the general superintendent of the line, to draw off the stock and abandon the road."

Indians seemed to be everywhere. On August 9, Bob Carson was killed while mowing hay near the Fort. Corriston, a young farmer, was killed. Three more wagon trains were robbed and burned. Six white men had been killed at Thirty-Two Mile Creek.

The Comstock family on the Little Blue in Nuckolls County had a call from Indians which they thought were friendly, but after having been well fed, the Indians turned and wounded several before they were driven away. Five miles east of the Comstock home at Oak Grove, Ulig, a boy about eighteen years old, was scalped and left to die on the prairie. But the Eubank story illustrated all that was dreaded by pioneer families.

The Eubanks were newcomers from the East and had no idea how to protect themselves from the Indians. They lived about four miles above Oak Grove at the Narrows on the Little Blue. There were two Eubank families at this ranch: William Eubank, Sr., his wife, two daughters, Hannah, twenty, and Dora, sixteen; two sons, James thirteen, and Henry, eleven. William, the oldest son, his wife and two children lived at the ranch. The elder William's wife and daughter Hannah were visiting in Iowa at the time of the raid.

Another son Joe lived about a mile west of Kiowa

station. Joe's brother Fred and Joe's brother-in-law, John Palmer, were staying with Joe. These three were making hay across the river from the Kiowa station. While Fred raked hay, Joe went down the river in search of more grass to cut. Palmer had gone back to the house.

A band of Indians shot Joe and took his pony. They moved up the river, killed Fred and took his horse. Another man named Kennedy, working nearby, was also killed. When Palmer returned to the hay meadow he found the men whose bodies were arrow-ridden and scalped.

Joe's father and brother James were returning from Joe's farm and were both killed. The ox team had been shot with arrows but escaped to be found seven days later, still alive.

That day, Laura Roper, whose father owned the ranch a mile and a half above the "Narrows," had ridden down with Mr. Kelly and Mr. Butler (who later were killed at the Comstock ranch) to spend the day with young Mrs. Eubank.

About four o'clock in the afternoon, young William, his wife, and two children left to take Laura home. Dora and the two other boys stayed at home. The women and children were sauntering down the trail, around a bluff, while William stopped to remove a sliver from his foot. When they heard yelling, they hurried back to Mr. Eubank, only to see him running toward his sister Dora who was being chased by Indians. Realizing that he could not save his sister, he turned and ran toward the river, but the Indians pursued and wounded him severely, and his body was found on a sandbar in the river. He, too, had been scalped.

The two small boys at the ranch attempted to escape up a small gully, but were killed. The Indians tried to take Dora prisoner, but she resisted and was killed with a tomahawk.

Meanwhile, Mrs. Eubank, Laura Roper and the two children, Isabelle, age four, and a baby boy about six months old, had hidden in a buffalo wallow. The Indians now started west toward the Roper ranch. The women had not been discovered and might have escaped, but little

129

Isabelle, frightened by all the commotion and the sight of Indians, began to scream. Their hiding place had been discovered!

The women were picked up and placed on horses and returned to the house. On their way back they had seen Dora's body beside the trail. Soon an Indian rode up yelling wildly with her scalp on his spear. This seemed to inflame those at the house, and they destroyed stoves, dishes, even the feather beds.

About six o'clock the women were placed on horses behind Indians and the party started south. They traveled all night. They rode on through the hot sun the next day and joined a second band of Indians that had captured extra horses. Now each woman was given a horse to ride. The second night Laura Roper's horse fell with her and Miss Roper broke her nose. One of the bucks wiped the blood from her face and painted her face with red paint and took her again on his horse.

A halfbreed who could speak English told them that the band were Cheyenne and Arapahoe. He also informed them that they would probably not be killed, but traded to other Indians.

Two more long weary days, stopping only for a few short rest periods, surviving on dried buffalo meat, except one wild turkey. By some miracle the baby and little Isabelle managed to survive. (Many early accounts of this event said that the baby had been killed, but Mrs. Eubank was fortunate to have her son with her during her long, weary captivity.) Miss Roper had been carrying Isabelle when they were captured, and the Indians, thinking that the child belonged to Miss Roper, would not let her be with her own mother.

About three o'clock on the fourth day, the little band joined another main camp. The women were turned over to the squaws, who nearly beat them to death. Here the women were separated, never to meet again. The baby went with the mother, and little Isabelle with Miss Roper.

On September 11, 1864 Major Wyncoop, commander at Fort Lyon, still influential with the Cheyennes, held a council with the Cheyennes and the Arapahoes on Hackberry Creek. By offering ransom, he was able to have Laura Roper, Isabelle Eubank and Dannie Marble, released to the soldiers. Laura Roper was returned to Nebraska Territory, later married and moved to Enid, Oklahoma. Little Isabelle Eubank was never returned to her relatives. Mollie Sanford stated that the little girl was adopted by a Dr. Brondsall in Denver, September 11. She died soon after.

Mrs. Eubank and her baby were not so fortunate. They were held by a band of Cheyenne who were not present at the council, and so were not released at that time.

TWO BOYS, ONE ARROW

Another dramatic attack took place near the Trail in Hall County. This story has become part of the folklore of the state. George Martin and his sons, Nathaniel, fourteen, and Robert, eleven, were making hay on their homestead twelve miles north of Juniata. They were almost ready to go home when nine Indians rode up. They attacked the father as he rode on the load of hay. He flattened himself in the hay and began to shoot his repeating rifle at his assailants. He shot and wounded one Indian and another's pony, so that Indian whirled about and made for the boys, who were about a quarter of a mile behind the father. The boys, seeing the skirmish, turned their ox team loose and jumped upon an old mare and headed for a little knoll where they might hide.

The other Indians continued to pursue the father, his hayrack and the frightened horses. One Indian, following behind the rack, shot an arrow that hit Mr. Martin in the neck, severing the jugular vein and lodging in his collarbone. When the horses and the careening rack passed near the house, Mr. Martin managed to drop off. Fortunately, Mrs. Martin and daughter Hepzibah had seen the rack coming, and the daughter grabbed a shotgun and held the Indians off while the mother dragged her husband into the house. It is said that she closed the wound and stopped the flow of blood by using a pin and horsehair.

Unfortunately, the boys were sighted when the Indians whirled about, and the mare who had a colt at the ranch headed for the barn. Arrows were flying all around them. One landed in Nathaniel's elbow. Another struck him in the back just under the shoulder blade near the backbone. It went through the right lung and came out below the right breast, sticking into Robert's backbone. The horse raced on, with the two brothers painfully pinned together. A third arrow grazed the older boy's hip, making a flesh wound, and stuck in Bob's hip. When the horse neared the house, the boys fell off. The fall caused the arrow to loosen from Bob's back. The blood continued to spurt from Nat's wound.

The Indians captured the horse and three came back to where the boys lay. Seeing the arrow through the older boy's body, they turned their attention to Bob. They hit him on the head several times to make certain that he was dead.

After the Indians were gone, the boys regained consciousness long enough to crawl to the barn out of the hot sun. With arrows still in them, weak from loss of blood and the shock of such an ordeal, they lapsed into unconsciousness.

Meanwhile, the family, seeing the boys being attacked, fled down the Trail toward Fort Kearny. But the next day they persuaded a party of freighters to go with them to recover the boys' bodies.

Much to their surprise and joy they found the boys alive. The four-inch arrowhead in the older boy's elbow was removed with a pair of shoeing pincers. The arrow that had pinned the boys together was pushed and drawn through Nat's body. The boys were loaded into a wagon and the family started to Nebraska City to the nearest doctor. But the bleeding started again from the jolting wagon, and the family returned to their home. The boys lingered between life and death for several days but miraculously recovered. It was almost a year before Nat could stand straight or work, but he lived to be 79 years old! Robert never entirely recovered from his back injury, although he lived for many years after this experience.

The Trail from Julesburg eastward was clotted with fleeing people. Some tried to take their stock and goods with them. Many ranches were abandoned, leaving stock and possessions unguarded. The fort at Kearny was crowded with refugees. The settlers at Grand Island decided to fortify their position and to stay. William Stolley had built a log house twenty-four feet square with twenty-five portholes, and some thirty-five people gathered there. Arms and ammunitions were stored, and preparations were made to hold off a prolonged attack. The O.K. store belonging to H. A. Koenig and F. A. Weibe was fortified with a breastwork of sod, and each corner was provided with a tower of cottonwood logs. An underground stable was built for their horses.

Back in the area around Fort Cottonwood, Widow Corriston brought a mare, a mule and 19 head of cattle to McDonalds for safekeeping. These were sold to the Quartermaster Corps on August 21. Herman Angell and the two Anderson brothers decided that the Indians had moved away from the vicinity of the Gilman ranch, so they went up into a pocket in the bluffs to bring in a load of hay. They took turns crawling to the top of the bluffs to inspect the surroundings lest the Indians surprise them. Herman went to the top of the bluff, and when he returned to the hay meadow he found both Andersons killed. He hid in a clump of bushes until dark and made it across the valley to the ranch. Herman had had enough excitement and had seen enough of the West, so he returned to Nebraska City on August 29, to resume the quiet occupation of shoemaking.

Excitement spread throughout the territory. Governor Saunders issued a call for volunteers for the state militia. Many loaded their guns, mounted their own horses and reported for duty. One regiment was formed from those north of the Platte River and one from south of the river. Among those who headed for the Trail was James Fitchie, the father of Mat Gilman, Jennie Fitchie, and Sam Fitchie. He was over fifty years old.

133

On August 17, the stage which had been halted at Cottonwood Springs pulled out for the East. Mrs. McDonald and her little son Willy left for Omaha to stay with her sister, Mrs. James Boyd. Martha, Jennie, and little George went to the safety of the Fitchie farm near Nebraska City.

Again mail service and freighting were halted. By the end of October, Plum Creek, Mullally's, Midway, Gilmans, Dan Smith's and Morrow's ranches had been garrisoned with small numbers of troops for escort duty. Detachments were sent to O'Fallon's Bluffs, Alkali, Beauvais ranch, and Julesburg. (Captain Charles Porter commanded 47 men at Gilmans.)

Colonel Robert R. Livingston assumed command of the road from Fort Kearny to Julesburg. O'Brien had been sent west from Cottonwood Springs, so he was replaced by Colonel S. W. Summers, also of the Seventh Iowa Volunteer Cavalry. Summers sent five telegrams to General Mitchell. One told of a storehouse erected by Gilmans at Fort Cottonwood; of trouble with Fitchie and Gilman's hired hand over wood being cut on an island near the Gilman fenced ranch; and needs for the fort at Cottonwood.

The mere presence of soldiers did not put out the Indian fires instantaneously. So desperate measures seemed necessary to Livingston. On October 17, he issued orders that the area south of the bluffs bordering the Platte Valley, on a line from Julesburg east to the Little Blue River be burned, making the area untenable to hostile Indians. The weather accommodated, and on October 22 a wall of flames moved from twenty miles west of Julesburg to ten miles east of Fort Kearny. A few scattered bands of Indians on hunting forays ran for their lives.

And still the attacks continued. Holladay's hay cutters were attacked at Midway on October 28. On November 5, guards drove off an attack at Sand Hill Station. On November 25, a stage coach was attacked near Plum Creek, two passengers were wounded and the telegraph wires were cut. When a stage coach was attacked after it left Midway, the seasoned old driver managed to outrun the pursuers and found shelter at Gilmans.

What happened at Sand Creek, Colorado on November 29, 1864 was a disaster not perpetrated by Indians this time. The government had ordered the peaceful Indians to separate themselves from the hostiles who were being hunted and punished. Black Kettle, a peaceful, intelligent Cheyenne chief, realized that bloodshed would never solve the problems. It is said that he and some other chiefs had asked for a peace council early in the fall but had been denied.

Both Cheyenne and Araphoes offered to exchange prisoners and to call off hostilities, but General S. R. Curtis, commanding the Department of Kansas, did not want to make peace. He believed it would be better to defeat them than give them survival rations promised by the government.

In the middle of October, Left Hand, the Araphoe chief, came to Fort Lyon returning some of the spoils from their summer raids. Major Scott J. Anthony, commanding officer there, being friendly to the Indians, gave them provisions and sent them to Sand Creek on the border of their reservation where he thought they would be safe. Soon these Indians were joined by Black Kettle, the Cheyenne, and his band. This village had about eight hundred Indians. They had an American flag flying over the chief's lodge to indicate that they had made peace.

In the later part of November, the camp received about two feet of snow. Colonel John M. Chivington, who had been a blacksmith, a preacher, and now an officer in the First Colorado regiment, had been recalled from the War between the States to help protect Colorado from Indian attacks. He was placed in charge of a militia regiment of volunteers who would serve for one hundred days.

It has been said that Chivington, acting on his own initiative, decided to put an end to the Indian problem. He led his volunteers, reinforced by 125 men from Fort Lyon, and strengthened by two cannons, to the Indian camp forty miles away. He ordered that no prisoners be taken, that all be killed. They surrounded the camp. Five hundred Indians were shot and scalped. Witnesses later said that Left Hand walked toward the troops with his hand raised in the traditional gesture of peace but was shot down. Ranchers applauded Chivington but easterners were shocked at such brutality.

No one could foresee the results of this unfortunate attack. As soon as the mourning ceremonials were completed the warpipe was carried as far as the Powder River to unite the Ogallalas, the Brules, and the Northern Cheyenne into a war party that would plague the plains for years to come. Not only the relatives of the Cheyenne, but Sioux, Apaches, Kiowa, Comanche, and even the mountain tribes of the Utes forgot their traditional differences and united into a force for revenge.

But Black Kettle, still the peace chief, gathered up the remainder of his band and moved farther south away from the shooting soldiers and his own angry young men. He would learn that General Custer did not bother to separate the hostiles from the friendlies. Next year Colonel Chivington would be brought to answer charges preferred against him.

Ben Holladay remembered Chivington with bitterness. The Colonel in charge of all Colorado, commanded that Holladay's stage line be moved from the Platte to the Lathan cut-off so it might be easier protected. The stations had already been stocked. It was estimated that the move cost Holladay, $80,000.

Snow came early everywhere in the plains. Jay Amos Barrett, an old freighter, wrote in his diary that he was caught in a snowstorm in the middle of November. They camped three nights, lost five steers, and ran out of fuel. They pulled into Gilmans when the weather cleared and stayed two nights.

It was sometime in December that those at the Gilman outer ranch saw a palace on wheels. Ben Holladay was on one of his inspection tours. This time he was attempting to determine the needs for the next season. Mr. Leland, a New

York hotel owner, had come along on this transcontinental trip.

The outside of the coach looked much like the other overland coaches except the trimmings were gold plate and tooled leather. The six white horses were the strongest and fastest on the line. The interior reflected all Ben's extravagance and imagination. There was a real mattress on the floor. Decorated kerosene lamps were suspended from the roof for night lighting. A little desk folded up against the end of the carriage and a storage cabinet contained the best liquor and cigars that money could buy. In spite of the cold winter weather, the two men rode up with the driver most of the time. Another coach traveling with them carried supplies, a cook, and personal servants. His elaborate coach was only one extravagance of the "stage king." Besides his palaces in the East, he had built a fabulous summer home at Lake Tahoe in the Sierra Mountains during the year.

According to the Post Returns sent to Headquartes by Captain Porter (The first report was dated October 31, 1864) the troops stationed at Gilman's Ranch did escort duty for wagon trains and stage coaches and made periodic scouting trips as far south as the Republican River. They sent scouts across the river to the north but did not find Indians. Since there were more troops than the ranch buildings could accommodate, the soldiers built a corral 150 feet long, one room 12 x 20 and one building for laundry quarters 28 x 16. They also cut and hauled 35 cords of wood from the canyons across the valley. Of course there were regular drills and duties around the Post. (December Post Returns)

The year 1864 finally ended. For the Gilmans as for all the ranchers from Fort Kearny to Julesburg, 1864 had been a year of heavy losses in profits and stock. However, all were thankful that they were still alive and Gilmans were grateful that their buildings were intact.

Chapter IX

1865
YEAR OF CONFUSION

If years could be assigned labels, 1865 might be called the year of confusion. The four-year, bloody Civil War ended, and thousands of veterans headed west, some to seek their fortune in the mines of California, Colorado or Montana, or to prospect in Idaho; others to file on homesteads; still others to fight Indians.

And there were plenty of opportunities to fight Indians. Nelson reported that about 30,000 Indians were on the warpath in this area, and, therefore, it was unsafe to continue to conduct "business as usual at the outer ranch, fifteen miles east of Cottonwood Springs. Most of the stock was moved up to the "branch establishment near the Fort." Gilmans and Sam Fitchie had fenced the area one half mile wide, one mile north taking in an island which lay north of the south channel of the Platte. Here the cattle could be contained, readily protected from the Indians, and available for trading or for butchering.

Indian retaliation for the Chivington massacre began on January 7 when they attacked Julesburg where one company of Seventh Iowa Cavalry was stationed. About a thousand Cheyenne and Arapahoes gathered in the hills near Julesburg. When they were sighted by scouts, about sixty soldiers were sent out to drive them away. But the Indians came forward, the soldiers were driven back and some of the best officers were killed. The Indians stayed outside of the range of the artillery at the post. Before dark, the Indians gathered up their dead and disappeared. It was thought that they were headed for the Republican River area southeast of Julesburg. If this were true some felt that Fort Cottonwood would be the next to be attacked. So General Mitchell ordered an expedition to conduct an Indian campaign.

Julesburg was reinforced by stage drivers and civilians in the vicinity, who determined to hold it against any attack. On January 15, Mitchell led 640 cavalrymen, taking with him artillery pieces; they searched the area where they supposed the Indians to have gone, but were only successful in having soldiers suffer from frostbite and hardships from weather. They returned to Cottonwood Springs on January 26. (Fifty of these were troops stationed at Gilman's ranch.)

But the Indians had not vanished. Scouts reported that it appeared that the Cheyenne, well armed with the best rifles, were about to move across the Platte to join the Northern Cheyenne who were somewhere in the Dakota country near Deadwood. On February 2, the warriors swooped down on Julesburg again, drove off cattle, burned the stage station, carried off a large quantity of corn and burned the row of haystacks near the stage station. The smoke from the haystacks hid a detachment of soldiers who had ridden up from Fort Cottonwood. These were able to enter the fort to help defend the area. The Indians attacked with fire arrows almost all night but by morning had again disappeared from sight.

The loss all along the valley was very great. It was estimated that Holladay's stage warehouse and station loss was $30,000. The painted savages burned stations and killed white men.

Captain Porter with 30 enlisted men from Gilmans' Ranch and under the command of Col. Livingston, U.S. Cavalry, proceeded by rapid march to the Julesburg area. When they arrived they were appalled by the destruction of property.

Captain Porter's company was sent up Pole Creek to

"ascertain the amount of damage done on the Pacific Telegraph line and to repair the same." The poles had been cut and carried away for seven miles. The company could not repair the line so they returned to Julesburg and a work party was sent out to replace the line.

Farther up along the line, 17 miles of line east of Pole Creek had been destroyed. Indians had taken or burned all the poles and carried part of the wire away.

Many ranchers were giving up and seeking safer places. Even Bob Williams, one of the oldest ranchers west of Cottonwood, in the vicinity of O'Fallons Bluffs, gave up and went back to Nebraska City and bought Vasser's Blacksmith Shop.

In spite of the many hit and run attacks, the raids on Julesburg, and the cold weather, trade resumed on the Trail by February. Roads were reopened to Denver. Cavalry units rode out from Fort Cottonwood in all directions to find and punish the Indians. The fortified ranches along the way provided escort for the freighting trains that had ventured out.

The soldiers at the Gilman Station continued to construct their post. The 150-foot corral wall constructed in the winter was extended and enclosed. It was 150 feet east and west, by 160 feet north and south. The new buildings were north of the Trail. They built stables for the horses along the north and west sides, and a gate facing the Trail, was about fifty feet from the southeast corner. The stage stable was along the outside of the corral between the gate and the southeast corner. Government hay was stacked north of the corral, while the stage company piled their hay on the west side of the post. About twenty-five feet south of the stage company's stables, a seven-room sod barracks housed the troops stationed there. These were about sixty feet north of the Trail. Nelson also described a fortification: "They built a fort underground, absolutely impregnable . . . the fort, which was about forty steps away from the ranch and consisted of a circular room some twelve feet in diameter, excavated in the ground, with an underground passage from it running to the stables. A stockade

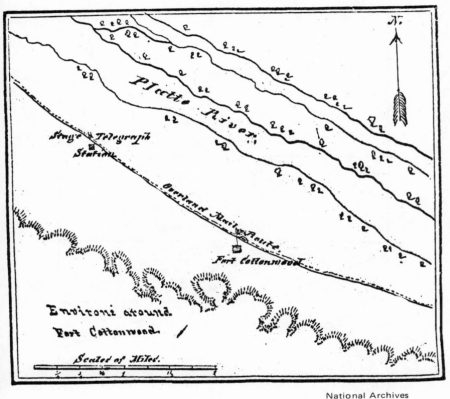

Plate showing military installations on the Oregon Trail, 1865 (from Sitgreaves papers)

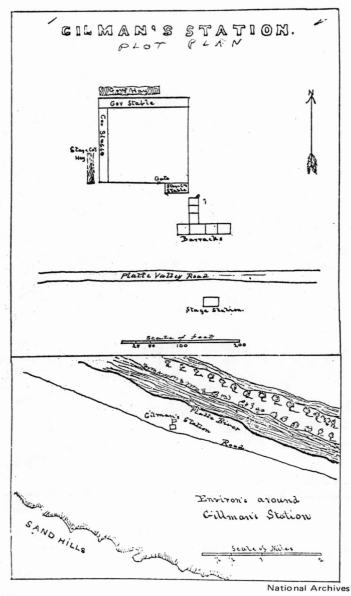

Plate showing military installations on the Oregon Trail, 1865 (from Sitgreaves papers)

142

surrounded it, absolutely impregnable, at least from attacks by Indians."

Charles Gaudreult of Gothenburg, Nebraska, an amateur archeologist, describes what he found of this structure when he was digging at the site. "Pit #3 was five foot deep or over, owing to the fact that the water table has raised in this part of the valley due to the fact that the Tri-County canal has brought the water level to within two and three feet of the surface. That is why I say over as we had to combat the water coming into the excavation and I know that the pit would be well over a man's head. This pit was eight feet long and five wide. It was lined with cedar logs which were burnt several feet beneath the top surface of the ground. There was a step faced with logs that would have raised a person high enough so that they could have looked over the top with ease. This pit faced the west and contained the barrels of a double barreled shotgun that had the left breech blown open. It was a muzzle loader and the ram rod was missing.

"Also a small cast iron brazer which I still have. Said pit had one Dr. Hostetter Stomach Bitters bottle and two other perfect bottles; also many broken ones. There were also empty cartridges."

These underground fortifications were often mentioned but few were described. General George A. Custer in his book *Life on the Plains* wrote of such a fortification between Fort Wallace and Fort Harker:

> To guard against such an emergency each station was ordinarily provided with what on the Plains is termed a dug-out. The name implies the character and description of the work. The dug-out was commonly located but a few yards from one of the corners of the stable, and was prepared by excavating the earth so as to form an opening not unlike a cellar, which was usually about 4' in depth, and sufficiently roomy to accommodate at close quarters half a dozen persons. This opening was covered with earth and loop-holed on all sides at a height of a few inches above the original level of the ground. The earth was thrown on top until the

143

dug-out resembled an ordinary mound of earth some 4' or 5' in height. To an outside observer, no means apparently were provided for egress or ingress; yet such was not the case.

About the middle of March, Jerome Dauchy, Gilman's old partner, stopped on his way back to Nebraska City. He had just gone through a hair-raising experience of having been arrested for shooting a desperado in Denver.

It required ingenuity to provide escorts for the trains and stages with only a small contingent of soldiers. On March 20, Eugene Scheffield, the post adjutant at Fort Cottonwood, was commanded to purchase some log buildings belonging to John Burke and S. D. Fitchie at Box Elder, two or three miles west of the Fort, to be used as shops, offices and quarters for soldiers. This added one more station to the west.

According to the official report given in the May 1865 Post Returns, real trouble occurred near the Gilman Station. The report said:

"May 12th. Company Sergeant Creighton and two men attacked by thirty Indians, five miles west of Smith's Station Nebraska Territory, fought the Indians four miles. Succeeded getting to Smiths station with the team, all of them wounded. Sergeant Creighton died that evening. Sergeant Creighton's horse killed. Two Indians and one Indian pony killed. Sergeant Lanstaff and four men fought the same band of Indians to two miles south of Smith's station. They had to fall back to the ranch to save themselves from being cut off. About a half mile from the station they made a stand, killed the leader of the Indians and captured his horse. Also killed two Indian horses. Sergeant Loomis (Frederick W. Lohmas), CN 1st Reg. Nebr. Vet Cal., wounded. Indians succeeded in driving off 20 head of cattle belonging to D. Smith. Capt. Porter with 26 mounted men from Gilman Station started in pursuit, succeeded in crossing the Platte River with 23 men, followed the Indians 15 miles to south fork of the Loup River. Before reaching them other parties had increased their number to about one hundred, followed them ten miles upstream when discovered where a large number of Indians had been in camp (about 3 or 4 thousand). There were some 40 campfires still burning. Concluded the Indians too numerous to follow without any chances of success and being 60 miles from any support, command returned to the Platte River and crossed in safety. Having traveled 170 in 51 hours and 60 miles of it each way without water."

The wounded from this skirmish were taken by surgeon Willey to the hospital at Fort Cottonwood. (In August of this year Private Frederick W. Lohmas was given the Congressional Medal of Honor for his bravery in this battle, at an elaborate ceremony at Fort Kearny. Governor Saunders and General Dodge were present.)

On June 10, 1865 Major George M. O'Brien, Seventh Iowa Cavalry, commanding Post Cottonwood reported to Captain George F. Price Acting Assistant Adjutant-General at Julesburg that stage stations between Fort Kearny and Julesburg had been supplied with troops.

The Indians were not intimidated. They continued to harass the ranchers, the travelers, and especially the telegraph line. The shining wire was no longer an object of superstition. Creighton was forced to keep crews constantly moving up and down the valley to keep the lines intact. Soldiers helped as much as they could.

Charles Whitehead, writing in the *San Francisco Chronicle* June 19, 1881, comments on the telegraph. He stated that Ed Creighton himself, with thirty-one men from the 11th Ohio Cavalry, patrolled the telegraph line. The Indians would gallop up to the line and throw a rope over the wire, start off in a gallop, tearing the wire from the poles. Bucks would light fires at the base of the poles.

All repairs had to be made at night. The soldiers would muffle their horses' hoofs with pieces of blankets. They padded their hammers, and rode without saddles. No talking was allowed, only whispers when absolutely necessary. Part of the men would dig new holes for the poles, insert the burning poles, making them secure while others drove large nails and hung the mended wire.

While they were doing this, Creighton himself undertook the most dangerous mission. He carried a spool of very thin wire covered with green silk and stretched it from one break to the other. The wire was suspended on sagebrush or weeds, sometimes broken by rabbits, bear or ponies. If Indians camped on the line, Creighton circled the camp. When he reached the break he would attach his pocket instrument and commenced to talk to Omaha or San Francisco, whichever the case might be. He also sent messages along the line. They counted on the fact that Indians seldom travel at night.

When the repair crew moved from place to place, they took ten wagons loaded with telegraph poles, proceeded in two lines with the men in the center between the wagons. If Indians were spotted the wagons corraled and the stock and men were inside the circle, and the poles were used as breastworks.

July and August came and the hay must be cut. The stations needed hay and the price was high, so every available man was hired to work the crews at the ranches. Each ranch had a few soldiers for guard duty, but the ranchers now hired them to help put up hay, paying them from $3 to $4 a day. (A complaint was registered at Post Cottonwood saying the post was short of men, and that the men at the small stations were working for the ranchers.)

Several events took place in August which the men at Gilman ranch would remember. General Dodge, one of the Union heroes of the Civil War, passed by on his way to Laramie. He stayed all night at Post Cottonwood and announced that he desired to change the name of the post. He would like to honor his good friend, Major General James B. McPherson, who was killed in action in July 1864 while commanding the Army of Tennessee in the battle for Atlanta. Since Dodge had political influence the change of name became official on February 26, 1866.

A soldier on his way back from Fort Laramie brought a copy of the August 19 *Union Vedette,* a newspaper published by the Fort Laramie Post, containing news of special interest to the Gilmans. According to the account, hostile Indians were camped about ten miles east of Laramie. Mr. Elston, in charge of the Indian village, took a party of Indian soldiers to investigate. He brought in two Chiefs and a white woman prisoner and her child. A Captain Palmer, who had talked to the captive, reported that it was Mrs. Eubank, and that a band of Cheyennes under Black Foot had captured her at her home on the Little Blue last fall. She and Miss Roper had suffered greatly before she had been purchased by Two Face, the Sioux. Their life under Two Face had been hard, but not as hard as with Black Foot. Palmer reported that Colonel Wyncoop had offered a ransom of $1,000 for Mrs. Eubank's return. Two Face had brought her in in response to negotiations for purchase.

But Colonel Moonlight reported to the editor of the paper that he made short work of these two chiefs. As soon as he found out who they were he hung them with trace chains in their cells. (Some day records may be found to tell the story of Two Face. The Omaha *Bee* newspaper insisted that he had captured Mrs. Eubank and had led the attacks in the Little Blue valley. He could scarcely have been there and at nearly the same time been outside of Fort Cottonwood. Other accounts say that Colonel Baumer hanged him at Fort Laramie because he had been a participant in the uprising. Those who knew him about the ranch believed that his was a profit motive. He had been a shrewd trader for the Gilmans but dependable in business dealings. There had been several occasions when he had warned the ranchers about war parties. Sharp, the scout, recalled an incident during the previous fall when Two Face had informed him that the families of the Brules were north of the river but the warriors were south.)

LEGAL PROBLEMS

In the telegram sent to General Mitchell on September 29, 1864, Colonel Summers had notified him of a contract for a log storehouse to be built by J. C. Gilman by October 15. A Captain John King was the Acting Quartermaster of

147

the U.S. Volunteers at Post Cottonwood at that time. The building was completed on time and accepted by the Post Commanding Officer but no payment was forthcoming. As William Russell, as Ben Holladay, and as Gilmans would later experience, it was one thing to do business with the federal government, especially the War Department, and it was another to collect what appeared to be owed.

The claim for the building, one for Isaac Coe for use of wagon, $96, and nine claims of O. P. Mason were submitted to the Quartermaster Department by D. J. McCann, a lawyer in Nebraska City. The claims were sent back with the directive to submit an affidavit of investigation. From the headquarters in St. Louis, inquiry was made to Captain Levi Ruggles, now stationed at Fort McPherson, to determine the value of the building, if the building had been necessary (in Post Cottonwood Returns, it was stated that Captain John King had been relieved of duty and directed under arrest to report to headquarters in Omaha on February 4, 1865), and if the building was in use and in the possession of the United States at this time.

It was fortunate that Captain Ruggles answered promptly:

Office A.A.Q.M.
Post Cottonwood, N.T.
October 24, 1865

"Respectfully returned to Brig. Gen. L. C. Easton Chf. Q.M. Dept. of Missouri. The building referred to was purchased for a Q.M. storehouse and is now in use as such. She is a good and substantial building framed and of logs and I would consider the price as a very reasonable one.

"The storehouse could not be dispensed with at this time and the purchase was without doubt necessary. The building is safe and spacious. The building could not be built at this time for less than three thousand dollars ($3,000.00.)

(Signed) Levi Ruggles
Capt. and
C.F.R.A.A.G.M.

There was much competition that year when the Quartermaster Corps advertised for hay. John Gilman and James LaForce drew up a contract and submitted it to Captain Ruggles, promising to furnish 1,000 tons of good hay to the Fort at the price of $49.75 a ton, but the Headquarters refused this price, and bought their hay from McDonald for $49.00 a ton.

A NARROW ESCAPE

The constant threat of marauding Indians made life on the Trail precarious. But Indians were not the only threat. Outlaws took advantage of the uprising to pillage and burn for their profit. Some of these men were outcasts drifting back from the mines in the west; others were deserters from the North or the South who were infesting the territory.

One morning soon after the hay crew had left for the hay "bottoms," Jerry and Johnny McBride were alone at the ranch house when two disreputable characters came riding into the ranch. It was evident that they had been sampling pilgrim whiskey. They brought their steaming horses up short and dismounted, almost falling in a heap before the door.

"Go to the cavalry barracks for help, Johnny," Jerry whispered.

Johnny slipped out and ran as fast as he could to seek help. Jerry went outside to meet the visitors, hoping to keep them from entering the store where they could do all kinds of damage. Both men were wearing the tattered Confederate caps of enlisted men. Deliberately they tied their horses to the hitching post and turned around. Each was carrying a brace of pistols.

Every trading ranch had a flagpole in front of the store. The flag, which was carefully raised and lowered every day, promised safety, rest, supplies or help, if needed..

One of the strangers, squinting his eyes aloft at the Gilmans' flag, said, "Yankee, take that rag down off that pole and give us a drink of good whiskey if you know what's good for you!"

Jerry walked slowly to the pump and offered them a drink of cool water, but that seemed to antagonize them. The other man turned his bleary eyes upward, pulled out both his guns, and grunted, "You heard what my partner sez. No damn Yankee flag's goin' to fly over me when I'm drinkin'!"

Jerry moved closer to the door of the store. Having no defense against four revolvers, he tried to delay as long as he could. "You must be tired from riding so hard," he remarked. The man with the guns pointed at him, fired a shot that made a hole in the door casing about three feet from Jerry's knees.

About that time a shot, seemingly from nowhere, grazed the man's arm. The sod-covered mound about forty steps from the ranch house porch, part of the newly constructed underground defense, had served its purpose. Both men whirled around. About that time four soldiers came from the stables, and soon both men were surrounded, and were given a military escort to a guardhouse up at the Fort where the Yankee flag continued to fly!

AN EXPENSIVE WOODPILE

When the war was over in the East, military units were released to serve on the frontier. Confederate prisoners had been allowed to volunteer for active duty along the trails. By the end of the year these "galvanized Yankees," as they were called, units of infantry, cavalry, and artillery, were scattered from the Missouri River to Montana. By October 18, Lieutenant M. B. Cutler had been sent on detached service from Fort McPherson to command a force of sixty-eight men (seven sergeants, one musician, and sixty corporal and privates) from Company A First Regiment Nebraska Volunteers at the Gilman Station. (Since last June, Gilman Station had been an outpost of Ft. McPherson.)

Winter began early, and many of these traveling units were forced to stay in tents, especially around the Fort.

From a long legal hassle over payment for damages which is recorded in the National Archives, it is known that United States troops under the command of Lieutenant Colonel Brown, 12th Missouri Cavalry, and Lieutenant Colonel R. C. Fleur, Engineers, 6th West Virginia Cavalry, while encamped on Gilman premises (which ranch is not indicated), burned seventy cords of wood and 2-1/2 miles of cedar fence for fuel. The original claim was witnessed by Ben Gallager and Jesse H. Lacy and submitted to R. C. Fleming, who was in command at the Fort at that time. The wood had been cut to fulfill another contract at Fort Sedgwick, and part of the wood had been delivered. The claim amounted to $1,440. Several law firms attempted to collect but were unsuccessful. In October 1870 the case was referred to Colonel Fleming, who responded, "There was some fencing burned by 168 forces for the within named party. As to the claim of $1,440 I never saw it before. The signature with certificate is mine, but I never gave it on that claim or to that amount. I have not been in Nebraska since 1868, and I know nothing of the claim Col. Brown of the 12th Missouri named, knows how much he burned, I presume."

But Colonel Brown did not answer the attorney's request for verification. In the letter summarizing all the legal correspondence over its payment, it was stated that "it was an apparent attempt to obtain payment of the claim by manufactured evidence, so it is entirely rejected. The manufactured evidence is explained as cutting off Col. Fleming's certificate from some other paper and attaching it to this claim."

Baldwin, the Gilmans' attorney at that time, and the Gilmans denied any knowledge of the manufactured evidence. Affidavits were presented which testified as to the integrity of the Gilmans. It was suggested that their agent, Mr. C. A. Downy, who was a drunkard and a refugee from justice, must have contrived this without their knowledge. There is correspondence which indicates that as late as 1873 payment had not been made.

John Nelson mentioned to O'Reilly that an expedition

organized to go out from Fort McPherson to pursue and punish the Indians was commanded by a Colonel Brown, a Confederate prisoner of war on parole. Was this the same Colonel Brown who refused to verify the Gilmans' claim when asked to do so?

In a book published in 1875, *Belden, The White Chief or Twelve Years Among the Wild Indians of the Plains,* edited by Gen. James S. Brisbin, there is an interesting anecdote of army life at the Gilman Station.

I was sent down from Camp Cottonwood (now Fort McPherson) with 30 men to Gilman ranch 15 miles east of Cottonwood on the Platte where I was to remain guard the ranch and furnish guards to the Ben Holliday (Holladay) overland coaches. In those days Gilmans was an important place and in earlier times had been a great trading post for the Sioux. Two or three trails led from the Republican to this place and every winter the Sioux had come in with their ponies loaded down with buffalo, beaver, elk and deer skins which they exchanged with the traders at Gilmans. War, however, put a stop to these peaceful pursuits, still the Sioux could not give up the habit of traveling these favorite trails. The ponies often came in from the Republican not now laden with furs, and robes, but each bearing a Sioux warrior. The overland coaches offered a great temptation to the cupidity of the Sioux, and they were not slow to avail themselves of any opportunity to attack them. The coaches carried the mail, much treasure and if the savages could now and then capture one they got money, jewels, scalps, horses and not infrequently, white women.

Troops were stationed in small squads at every station, about ten miles apart, and they rode from station to station on top of all coaches, holding their guns ever ready for action.

Among the soldiers stationed at Gilman's Ranch were a number of Omaha and Winnebago Indians, who belonged to my company, in the First Nebraska Cavalry. I had done all I could to teach them the ways of civilization, but despite my instructions, and their utmost endeavours to give up their wild and barbarous practices, every now and then old habits would become too strong upon them to be borne, and they would indulge in the savage customs of their youth. At such times they would throw aside their uniforms, and, wrapping a blanket about them, sing and dance for hours.

One evening they were in a particularly jolly mood, and having obtained permission to have a dance, went out in front of the building, and for want of a better scalp-pole, assembled around one of the telegraph poles. One fellow pounded lustily on a piece of leather nailed over the mouth of a keg, while the others hopped around in a circle, first upon one leg, then the other, shaking over their heads oyster cans that had been filled with pebbles, and keeping time to the rude music, with a sort of a gutteral song. Now it would be low and slow, and the dancers barely moved, then, increasing in volume and rapidity, it would become wild and vociferous, the dancers walking fast, much as the Negroes do in their cake walks. We had all manner of dances and songs, and enough drumming and howling to have made any one tired, still the Indians seemed only warming up to their work. The savage frenzy was upon them, and I let them alone until near midnight. Their own songs and dances becoming tiresome, I asked them to give me some Sioux songs, for I had been thinking all the evening of the village up the Missouri, and of my squaws. The Indians immediately struck up a Sioux war song, accompanying it with the war dance.

All the Indian songs and dances are terminated with a jump, and a sort of wild yell or whoop. When they had danced the Sioux war song, and ended it with the usual whoop, what was our surprise to hear it answered back at no great distance, out upon the prairie. At first I thought it was the echo, but Springer, a half-breed Indian, assured me what I had heard was the cry of other Indians. To satisfy myself I bade the Indians repeat the song and dance. And this time, sure enough, when it was ended the whoop was answered quite near the ranch. I went inside, lest my uniform should be seen, and telling Springer to continue the dance, I went to a back window and looked out, in the direction from which the sound came.

The moon was just rising, and I could distinctly see three Sioux Indian warriors sitting on their ponies, within a few hundred paces of the house. They seemed to be intently watching what was going on, and were by no means certain as to the character of the performers or performance. At a glance, I made them out to be our deadly enemy, the Ogallalla Sioux, and determined to catch them. I quickly called Springer, and bade him kindle up a small fire, and tell the Indians to strike up the death song and scalp dance of the Sioux. This, as I expected, at once reassured the strange warriors, and, riding up quite close, they asked Springer, who was not dancing, and who had purposely put himself in their way:

"What are you dancing for?"

"Dancing the scalps of four white soldiers we have killed," replied Springer.

"How did you kill them?" inquired the foremost Indian warrior.

"You see," said Springer, who, being part Sioux, spoke the language perfectly, "we were coming down from the Neobarrah (Niobrara) and going over to the Republican to see Spotted Tail and our friends, the Ogallallas, when some soldiers fired on us here, and seeing there were but four of them, we attacked and killed them all. They are now lying dead inside; come, get down and help dance their scalps."

Two of the warriors immediately dismounted, giving their ponies to a third one to hold, who remained mounted. Springer seemed to take no notice of this but leading the warriors up to the dance, joined in with them, the other Indians making room in the circle for the newcomers.

When the dance ended, Springer said, "Come, let us bring out the scalps!" and turning to the two Indians, inquired, "Will you look at the bodies?" About half the Indians had already gone into the ranch, under pretense of getting the scalps, and the two Sioux walked in with Springer, apparently without suspicion that anything was wrong.

As soon as they had crossed the threshold the door was closed behind them, and two burly Omahas placed their backs against it. It was entirely dark in the ranch, and Springer proceeded to strike a light. When the blaze of dry grass flared up it revealed everything in the room, and there stood the two Sioux, surrounded by Omahas, and a dozen revolvers leveled at their heads.

Never shall I forget the yell of rage and terror they set up, when they found they were entrapped. The Sioux warrior outside, who was holding the ponies, heard it, and plunging his heels into the sides of his pony, made off as fast as he could. Notwithstanding my men fired a dozen shots at him he got off safely, and carried away with him all of the three ponies.

The Sioux in the ranch were bound hand and foot, and laid in one corner of the room; then my Indians returned to the telegraph pole to finish their dance. Feeling tired, I lay down and fell asleep.

Next morning I was awakened by the most unearthly yells, and looking out, saw my Indians leaping and dancing and yelling around the telegraph pole, where they now had a large fire burning. Presently Springer came in and said the Indians wanted the prisoners. I told him they could not have them, and that in the morning I would send them to Colonel Brown at McPherson, as was my duty. Springer, who was a non-commissioned officer, communicated this message to the Indians, and the yelling and howling redoubled. In a short time, Springer came in again, and said he could do nothing with the Indians, and they were determined to have the prisoners, at the same time advising me to give them up. I again refused, when the Indians rushed into the ranch, and seizing the prisoners, dragged them out. Seeing they were frenzied I made no resistance, but followed them closely, keeping concealed, however.

They took the Sioux to an island on the Platte, below the ranch, and there, tying them to a tree, gathered a pile of wood and set it on fire.

Here follows a description of the unspeakable tortures which the unfortunate prisoners suffered, and which are too horrible to be told in these pages.

The Sioux uttered not a complaint, but endured all their sufferings with that stoicism for which the Indian is so justly celebrated, and which belongs to no other race in the world.

Sick at heart, I crept back to the ranch and went to bed, leaving the Indians engaged in a furious scalp dance, and whirling the bloody scalps of the Sioux over their heads, with long poles to which they had them fastened.

Next morning, when I awoke, I found the Indians wrapped in their blankets, and lying asleep all around me. The excitement of the night had passed off, and brought its corresponding depression. They were very docile and stupid, and it was with some difficulty I could arouse them for the duties of the day. I asked several of them what had become of the Sioux prisoners, but could get no other answer than, "Guess him must have got away."

I was sorely tempted to report this affair to the commanding officer at Fort McPherson and have the Indians punished, but believing it would do more good in the end to be silent, I said nothing about it. After all, the Omahas and Winnebagoes had treated the Sioux just as the Sioux would have treated them, had they been captured, and so it being a matter altogether among savages I let it rest where it belonged.

So 1865 ended as it began, a year of terror, uncertainty, high prices, severe weather, bloodshed and homesick men separated from their families. The president had been assassinated. Mrs. Morton, who had been captured at Plum Creek in August 1864, was ransomed at Fort Laramie and returned to her home in Iowa during March.

But there were a few bright spots. A treaty had been signed by Spotted Tail and Man-Afraid-of-His-Horse at Laramie. The Union Pacific Railroad was now forty miles west of Omaha. There was still romance. Sam Fitchie, Mat Gilman's brother, married William Baker's daughter, Ruhamah. Jerry Gilman was still a bachelor, but he made an attempt to drive out to the Fitchie home on Camp Creek every time he went to Nebraska City.

Chapter X

1866
IRON WHEELS ACROSS THE PRAIRIE

With the prospect that the railroad would soon be built across Nebraska and with more soldiers on the frontier, the settlers were optimistic. The soldiers stationed at the Fort and the families around the Post celebrated the New Year with a New Year's Ball at McDonalds. The music was lively, the ladies dressed in their best ruffles and bustles, the soldiers in uniform and sash, the boots, spit and polished. For a few hours the storeroom was warmed with laughter, in corners where heat from the iron stove could not reach.

Many changes would come to the Trail this year. Holladay was still trying to get the stage line back on schedule. His losses were great and prices were high, so he submitted his claim for damages suffered during 1865, to Congress for payment. The itemized account totaled $529,090. The amount of grain destroyed at Gilmans was listed as thirty sacks of grain (3,360 pounds) at twenty cents a pound, or $672. At Midway it was estimated that thirty sacks of corn, fifteen tons of hay, and dishes and furniture totaled $1,772. As would be expected, this resulted in a long-drawn-out squabble and the government never fully reimbursed Holladay for his losses.

By October 1866, Ben Holladay made a decision. As the Union Pacific tracks were laid at an unimagined rate across Nebraska, Ben could see that his stage-coaching empire would soon disappear. A competitor, Butterfield's Overland Dispatch, on the Smoky Hill Route through northern Kansas, was making three trips a week, and the route was seventy miles shorter. Wells Fargo Express Company, which had been growing more powerful in the West, now threatened to stock the Butterfield Line. If this happened Ben's crippled line would be doomed. So in October he made a deal to sell all his stage holdings to Wells Fargo for $1,500,000 plus $500,000 worth of feed and provisions, and take $300,000 worth of Wells Fargo stock and seat on the board of directors.

So from now on, the stages flashing by between railroad terminals would carry the famous Wells Fargo insignia. Ben now turned his attention to the big gamble—railroads in western states. But he soon learned the bitter lesson that Russell, Majors, Waddell, Horace Tabor and others of this era had also learned: that fortunes could be made, that luxury could be bought and empires built, but they could also disappear much more quickly than they were constructed.

Editors of territorial papers wrote columns about the problems of reconstruction in the South, but among the ranchers the one common topic of conversation was Indians. While Spotted Tail and Man-Afraid-of-His-Horses signed the Harney-Sanborne Treaty in 1865, Red Cloud did not. He was recuperating from a critical wound caused by a Crow arrow. He was not in agreement with the provisions which allowed the white man free movement across Sioux territory to the new mines in Montana. Young warriors who followed him continued to harass the stagecoaches, trains and settlements.

As early as February 1866, plans were made to send out the second treaty commission to offer the Sioux new terms. Runners spread out from headquarters and the Indian agencies throughout the territories, inviting all the northern tribes to meet for council at Laramie as soon as the grass was high enough to feed the ponies. The terrible punishment these bands of Indians had taken, the hard winter, and the lack of food must have caused the chiefs to regard this invitation favorably. Travelers and ranchers along the Trail were hopeful that the trouble with Indians now would end.

A GRAVE ON STILTS

John Nelson had not seen his old friend Spotted Tail for some time, so when the dramatic accounts of the burial of his daughter filtered down from Fort Laramie the men at the ranch questioned every traveler from the West concerning the story.

Nelson told again and again how he had wandered into Spotted Tail's tepee when he first ran away from the wagon train which brought him to the territory; how he was adopted into the tribe and given the name Cha-sha-sha-opog-geo or "Redwood-Fill-the-Pipe" because he enjoyed smoking ground up red willow twigs mixed with plug tobacco; and that Nelson's first squaw had been Spotted Tail's niece.

Road ranchers often fed the bands as they passed the ranch headquarters in order to keep trade relations friendly. Gilmans had traded with the chief's tribe and had been impressed with his good business judgment and his apparent wise leadership.

Spotted Tail was well known by both ranchers and soldiers at Fort Cottonwood and Fort Laramie. He was the head chief of the Brule (Sioux) tribe—a warrior recognized for his bravery in battle and his wisdom in councils. It is said that he participated in the Grattan massacre and the battle at Ash Hollow. He was captured and served time in the Federal penitentiary at Leavenworth. After the last council he had moved his band away from the Trail to the Powder River country of Montana.

It is not known just how much of the story of Spotted Tail's daughter the Gilmans and Nelson were able to learn for it caught the imagination of many white people and was told and retold for years after. Historians have argued about her name. Eugene Ware called her Ah-ho-appa (Wheat Flower); Susan Bettelyoun, a half-breed, who had lived at Fort Laramie, called her Minniakurrin or Hinzmwin; Simonin, a French mining engineer, called her Moneka; others called her White Flower, Falling Leaf or Mini-aku, so called by George Colhoff, of the Pine Ridge Reservation in a letter dated October 28, 1898. Dr. Wilson O. Clough of the Wyoming Historical Society, after having examined all the known sources of her story, concluded that Mini-aku, meaning Brings Water, was the most likely name.

The following summary of the burial of Spotted Tail's daughter is based on the account as given by Eugene Ware, Colonel Henry A. Maynadier, commanding officer at Fort Laramie, at the time, and Chaplain Wright's account which appeared in the St. Louis *Democrat.*

All Sioux had great affection for their children, but Spotted Tail had an unusual daughter for whom he had unusual affection. Elton, the Indian agent at Laramie, remembered her as a baby in the squaw camp near Fort Laramie. As she grew up, she was very different from the other Indian girls. She was proud and strong, and carried a knife. Many young bucks had wanted to marry her but she swore that she would never marry an Indian, only a "captain," meaning a soldier in uniform.

She had tried to learn to speak English from a captured white boy but he escaped before she succeeded. She seemed always to carry with her a little Episcopal prayerbook bound in red leather which General Harney was said to have given her mother. She would not learn to do an Indian woman's work around the camp, but dressed like a young buck, handled a gun, and went with her father whenever he went where the white men were.

Those who knew who she was, called her "Princess." When they were at Fort Laramie she always stood apart, watching the guard mount in the morning and dress parade at night. She asked no questions and showed no emotion at what she saw.

Soldiers at the Fort believed that she had last seen a white person in August 1864, for after that Spotted Tail took his camp up on Powder River. Men theorized that she had contracted tuberculosis, or pneumonia from exposure to the extreme weather, or suffered some other type of lingering disease. In her illness, she still yearned to see white man's houses and his way of life.

When the runner came to invite Spotted Tail to the Laramie Council, the girl was dying. She told her father that she wished to go to Laramie once again, but that she knew she would be dead before the Council. Would her father take her to be buried beside their relative, Old Smoke, in the soldiers burial ground? Before she died she also asked Spotted Tail to promise her that he would kill no more white men.

At her death Spotted Tail sent a runner to the Fort to ask permission to bring his daughter in for burial. The squaws had wrapped her body tightly in smoked deerskin (which temporarily embalmed). Her two white ponies were tied together to carry Mini-aku for the two hundred and sixty mile journey.

Down the bleak, frozen, mountainous trail for fifteen days Spotted Tail and his family followed the two white ponies to the little settlement on the level land near the junction of the Laramie and North Platte Rivers.

From Maynadier's report to D. N. Cooley, Commissioner of Indian Affairs:

"Yesterday I was informed that he (Spotted Tail) had reached the Platte River and would soon be at the fort. Wishing to do him honor as being one of the principal chiefs of the nation and on account of the peculiar circumstances of his visit, I rode out with several officers and met him halfway between the fort and the Platte. After greeting him, I conducted him to the fort and to my headquarters. I then informed him that the Great Father offered peace to the Indians, and desired them to have it for their own benefit and welfare. That, in two or three months, commissioners would come to treat with them and settle everything on a permanent basis of peace and friendship. I sympathized deeply in his affection, and felt honored by his confidence in committing to my care the remains of a child

161

whom I knew he loved much. The Great Spirit had taken her, and he never did anything except for some good purpose. Everything should be prepared to have her funeral at sunset, and as the sun went down it might remind him of the darkness left in his lodge when his beloved daughter was taken away; but as the sun would surely rise again so she would rise, and someday we would all meet in the land of the Great Spirit.

"The chief exhibited deep emotion during my remarks, and tears fell from his eyes, a rare occurrence in an Indian, and for some time he could not speak. After taking my hand, he commenced with the following eloquent oration: 'This must be a dream for me to be in such a fine room surrounded by such as you. Have I been asleep during the last four years of hardship and trial and dreaming that all is well again, or is this real? Yes, I see that it is; the beautiful day, the sky blue, without a cloud, the wind calm and still, to suit the errand I come on and remind me that you offered me peace. We think we have been much wronged and are entitled for compensation for the damage and distress caused by making so many roads through our country, and driving off and destroying the buffalo and game. My heart is very sad, and I cannot talk on business; I will wait and see the counsellors the Great Father will send.'

"Preparations were then made for the funeral of the chief's daughter. A scaffold was erected at the cemetery and a coffin made. Just before sunset the body was carried to the scaffold, followed by her father and mother and other relatives, with the chaplain, myself and other officers, and many of the soldiers of the garrison, and many Indians. Amid profound silence, and, I was glad to see, with most devout and respectful behavior on the part of every white man present, the chaplain delivered a touching and eloquent prayer, which was interpreted by Mr. Gott. I can hardly describe my feelings at witnessing this first Christian burial of an Indian, and one of such consideration in her tribe. The hour, the place, the solemnity, even the restrained weeping of her mother and aunts all combined to affect anyone deeply."

162

FROM THE DESK OF:

Musetta A. Gilman

Thank you for the book order.
I do hope that you can attend the
O.C.T.A. meeting in Scottsbluff
next summer.

Sincerely,

Musetta

As to the preparation which the Colonel mentioned, Ware added that the Indian women wrapped a bright red blanket around the deerskin shroud and placed the body in the coffin. The Colonel placed a pair of beautiful new gauntlets to keep her hands warm. Others added little gifts. Spotted Tail stood silently, then handed the little red prayer book to the Chaplain who laid it carefully in her coffin. A scaffold of twelve-foot poles tied together by thongs, was erected near Old Smoke's grave, and a buffalo robe was thrown over the scaffold on which the coffin was placed. A fresh buffalo hide was laid over the coffin and securely fastened down with rawhide thongs which would grow tighter as they dried. Her two white ponies had been killed and the heads and tails nailed to the poles, so that after death they might carry her through the fair hunting grounds of the sky.

But all too soon other army officers would come not seeking peace nor being sensitive to the concerns of the Indians. The long iron rails were cutting through Sioux country with alarming speed, and the blood of both White and Red would stain the ground on which Mini-aku had wandered in search of her "captain."

But the War Department was trying to reduce the armed forces. By April 2, seven companies of Iowa Cavalry under the command of Major J. Wilcox left Fort McPherson and camped near the Gilman ranch. The men were in a festive mood, for they were on their way to Fort Leavenworth and many were being mustered out to return to civilian life.

On April 10, the company of soldiers who had been stationed at the Gilman ranch and other stations along the Trail, left the posts. Was the Indian trouble really over?

CARRINGTON TO PINEY WOODS

General Henry B. Carrington, referred to by his enemies as a civilian general, had been transferred to Fort Kearny in 1865. (He was a colonel in the regular army.) In the spring

163

of 1866 he was ordered to take troops to the West and set up headquarters at new Fort Reno. He was to take 220 men from the Second Battalion, 18th United States Infantry, and a supplement of new recruits. There was no cavalry to accompany them, but they were to pick up 200 horses at Laramie to mount the infantry.

It was an impressive cavalcade that started up the Trail from Fort Kearny on May 19. Carrington was taking 226 mule-team outfits besides a thirty-piece band (armed) and ambulances carrying the families of several army officers.

Carrington was determined to take some evidences of civilization with him. Mrs. Carrington had packed her best chairs, bed, mattress, potatoes, groceries, and fifty dried beef tongues for the new home, but unfortunately, their house burned just before departure. However, they did take turkeys, chickens and some pigs to start flocks and herds in the wilderness. The wagons were also loaded with machinery of all kinds. They took mowing machines, doors, window sashes, glass, nails and locks, and picked up an idle sawmill at Fort McPherson. Jim Bridger and H. Williams guided the expedition. The soldiers marched every day but Sunday.

On May 23, the soldiers camped at Gilmans'. The officers and their ladies were offered hospitality at the ranch. Mrs. Carrington wrote in her book *Ab-Sa-Ra-Ka* that they had been entertained at these ranches along the way from Fort Kearny to Cottonwood Springs: "Gallager; Pat Mallalley; Dan Smith; Gilman, a man of business, straightforward and worthy; and by Coles." Beyond Fort McPherson, she mentioned Fitchies, Burkes, Morrow, Baker, Brown, Beauvois, and Valentines. She was especially impressed with Jack Morrow. "We stopped to speak with Jack Morrow, a prince of ranchmen and king of good fellows."

What a sight this must have been—columns of marching men over dusty trails, the mule trains pulling the groaning wagons of supplies, the swaying ambulances with army wives trying to adjust to the discomforts of the Trail, including swarms of buffalo gnats! The herd of bellowing, lumbering cattle was followed by mounted guards bringing up the rear.

CALAMITY AT THE COUNCIL

It is presumed that Carrington knew of the Indian Council being held at Fort Laramie. Members of the tribes had been congregating for several weeks. Chiefs and soldiers smoked the peace pipes and details for the new treaty were about completed, when around June 17, Carrington with his troops arrived at the scene. Red Cloud was furious. He declared that Carrington had come to steal the road through their land. He gathered his band together and left, which broke up the council. Other chiefs followed him.

Red Cloud became the great leader of the Sioux, and was instrumental in uniting the opposition to white man in this area. Crazy Horse, Black Shield and High Backbone joined him in this effort. The Sioux gathered from all over the region. It is said that their encampment extended for many miles up and down Little Goose River. An estimated four thousand fighting men and as many as fifteen thousand Indians were lined up against Carrington and his force, whose task was to build two new forts—Fort Phil Kearny on Piny Creek, and a second post ninety-one miles north to be named C. F. Smith. The forts were to protect the Bozeman Trail.

From the very beginning these Indians threatened the civilian crews hired to cut timber, and soldiers on patrol duty. Attacks became more frequent and bolder as the summer moved into fall, and reached a climax in December.

Little is known about the activity around the Gilman ranch in the first part of 1866. The hazards of the Trail were too great to send the freighting trains to Denver or to Salt Lake City. Billy Campbell and his brother, John, did haul government supplies.

Jerome Dauchy was living back in Nebraska City. (Herman Angell had not returned to the West after his narrow escape in 1864.) Ben Gallager, who had been the official sutler (storekeeper) at Fort McPherson, left to become a merchant in the new town of Cheyenne. William Cody, who had been driving stage on Bill Trotter's division since last year, left in February and went back to St. Louis and was married on March 6.

One thing is recorded. John Nelson had been scouting for the army. After the news that treaties had been made with some of the tribes in the fall of 1865, he decided to try his luck at trading again with the Indians.

JOHN NELSON TRADES AGAIN

The Gilmans wanted me to go out with an outfit, but they did not care to undertake the risk in their own account. I therefore offered to embark in the speculation, provided they would give me something to go on credit. This they did to the tune of $3,275 and for it I obtained a wagon, six yoke of oxen, and the stock I needed.

With this I went down south to meet the Indians returning from Laramie, and struck them at Medicine Creek, about eighteen miles south of Fort McPherson.

Here I met my squaw, and found that during my absence she had presented me with a daughter, who was then over twelve months old. We were glad to meet again and I took her and the child into my outfit. The Indians could not stay to trade, as they were bound for the Republican River to meet a larger band of Sioux coming up from the south. It was arranged that we should follow on, and join them at the mouth of the Stinking Water River, about one hundred and fifty miles distant.

The winter at this time had fairly set in, the snow was over three feet deep, and we had great difficulty in making our way through it. Often I had to work hard all day shoveling the snow away, and at night I would not have made more than a mile progress.

My outfit consisted of six people—i.e. my squaw and

the child, myself, two teamsters, and a young Indian boy, about ten years of age, whom I had adopted and christened "Jo."

I shall always remember that winter, for it was the coldest I ever experienced. In a gulch that we passed we came across more than three hundred buffalo that had been frozen to death. All were as hard and immovable as if carved out of rock. I killed many deer and elk whilst they were fixed in the snowdrifts, and thus kept our larder supplied.

In February the snow suddenly disappeared, but the streams were very high, and we had to wait a long time on the banks before we could cross them.

One day my Indian boy, who had been watching on a hill, came running into camp and reported that a war party was in sight. We hardly had time to make preparations when they swooped down and surrounded us. There were seventy-five of them, and they were Cheyenne "dog soldiers" who had come from southern Kansas, where they had been fighting the colored troops sent out to protect that part of the country.

The party was on their way north to the Platte River to intercept the caravans coming along the Denver route to Julesburg. We were not anxious for a fight against such long odds, but we got our guns out and waited for them to open the ball.

Jennie went out to talk to them, as they all knew her, and ascertained that they knew nothing about the treaty of peace and were still on the warpath. As the chief, however, expressed a desire to see me, she bade him lay down his arms and come into our tepee to have an interview.

This he did, and came in with his blanket over his head, in Indian fashion. I stood in the center of the tepee with my rifle in my hand, and on my right stood the two teamsters with their guns, whilst the boy was behind us with a six shooter in each hand.

When the chief took his blanket from off his head I at once recognized him as White Antelope, into whose camp I had inadvertently run some time previously.

As he was a brave of great influence with his tribe I

lit my pipe of peace and offered it to him, but he refused to smoke with me.

John and his outfit were saved for a short time by the appearance of Lone Wolf, a Sioux, Jennie's brother, but they were held by the Sioux for six months. When a force of some eighty soldiers under Captain Egan was about to attack the Sioux in retaliation for a Cheyenne raid, Nelson was able to warn the captain that the Sioux had about 1,500 warriors in ambush. The cavalry retreated back to the fort without a skirmish. For no apparent reason the Nelson party was released and allowed to go back to the ranch.

Nelson concluded this story by saying that he returned the unsold stock to the Gilmans but still made a profit of several hundred dollars from his trading. Since there was nothing to do at the ranch, he went up to Fort McPherson and worked as a scout, guide, and interpreter going with the men who were repairing the telegraph lines under guard.

RAIL RHYTHM

Big news was tapped out on the telegraph wires in May. General Dodge had resigned his command with the army, and had become the chief engineer for the Union Pacific Railroad Company. John Gilman always had his ear open for new economic sounds. He heard of the opportunity to supply teams and wagons. Certainly there would be a demand for good cedar logs for ties and bridges as the shining rails extended westward. Just how the Gilman oxen, wagons, and scrapers became involved with the Union Pacific is not known. It is interesting to note that as early as April 24, 1865 John Gilman had registered at the Herndon House in Omaha, a popular place for anyone involved with big business or with politics. John Gilman possessed Pass #1 issued by the Union Pacific which allowed him to ride trains without purchasing tickets, so he must have been one of the first to be involved. (This pass is still prized by John's granddaughter.)

As was mentioned before, only forty miles of track had

168

been laid west of Omaha by the end of 1865. By August 1866 trains were moving as far west as Fort Kearny; and by the end of the year, North Platte near the junction of the North and South Platte rivers would be "Rail's End."

What a spectacular sight the building of the railroad must have been along the Platte Valley north of the river. General Jack Casement, a prominent brigade and division commander, during the Civil War, and his brother Dan, were the general construction contractors. Both were slight of stature, but were once called "the little giants" because they had unusual abilities in working with men and materials to get the rails laid across the country.

Later, General Dodge described the building pattern. Every step was carefully planned. The surveying party, accompanied by soldiers in Indian country, were able to cover from eight to twelve miles a day. In mountains it generally took a day to survey one mile.

Then came the army of construction workers. Imagine 10,000 graders, woodcutters, bridge builders, and track layers. Ten thousand animals and two thousand graders covered one hundred miles in thirty days.

General Jack Casement himself supervised the actual laying of the rails, after this battalion of sweating men moved tons of dirt day after day until the long black ridge of the track bed stretched as far as the eye could see. The bridge builders managed to stay about twenty miles in front of the track layers.

Bases for supplies were established at Fremont, Fort Kearny, North Platte and later Julesburg, Sidney, Cheyenne, and Laramie. At these bases, large tent towns mushroomed. Miles of siding were put in for switching. Shops and sometimes roundhouses were built. In this tent city, gamblers, saloon keepers, traders, and crude eating establishments flourished for a short time, then the population would move on to the next base.

Beside the track, telegraph lines were built. The work crews at the "end-of-track" could keep in touch with the

Union Pacific track layers at work

headquarters in Omaha, unless the Indians decided to cut the precious wire.

For those living along the south side of the river, the coming of the railroad brought great changes. Peniston and Miller, who had operated Cold Water ranch (Smith's east ranch), it is said, had gone back East to bring their brides back to Nebraska. Stopping in Nebraska City, they left the ladies at the home of J. Sterling Morton while they came on out to check the ranch. Before they arrived, the Indians had burned the buildings. So they salvaged what they could, and moved to North Platte to open up the first permanent store there.

POLITICS

As far back as 1860, there had been agitation for taking the necessary steps to form a Nebraska state constitution, which might be acceptable to Congress. This proposition was submitted to a vote on March 5, 1860, but was defeated because the people felt they were too poor and taxes were already too high. But on July 28, 1866 Congress voted to admit Nebraska as a state, but it was near the end of the session, and President Johnson did not sign the bill so it lost as a "pocket veto."

However, there were local elections. Shorter County (later Lincoln County) had elected officials in 1860 but little business was conducted. Andreas in his *History of Nebraska* stated that J. A. Morrow and Charles McDonald were the only ones who had taken the trouble to qualify for office. Judge McDonald did perform some marriage ceremonies and that was possibly the extent of the political activities until 1866.

On September 3, a meeting was held at Cottonwood Springs to reorganize the county. It was decided to name the county in honor of the martyred president. This time the following officers were elected: County Commissioners—J. C. Gilman, W. M. Hinman, and J. A. Morrow; Judge—S. D. Fitchie; Sheriff—William Baker; Clerk—Charles McDonald.

171

Territory of Nebraska
Lincoln County.

At a meeting of the Board of County Commissioners within and for said county On Monday the first day of October A.D. 1866 there being present and acting W M Hinman & J C Gilman Commissioners, at Cottonwood Springs being the first meeting of Commissioners court after the organization of said Lincoln County in said Territory of Nebraska, the following business was transacted

It was ordered by the said Board that said Lincoln County be divided into three commissioners districts as follows, to wit

All that portion of Lincoln County lying east of Moran Cañon, commonly known as four Mile canon, and west of a certain Ravine known and described as Snake ravine which crosses the main road immeadiately east of Wright and Jeffries ranch Shall be known and designated as District No. one. All that portion of said County lying east of said Snake ravine and the eastern boundary of said Lincoln County Shall be known and designated as District No two And all that portion of said County lying west of said Moran or four mile canon and east of the Western boundary of said County shall be known and designated as District No three

On Motion Board adjourned to meet at Cottonwood Springs in said County on Tuesday the 2nd day of Oct 1866.

Chas McDonald
County Clerk

Minutes of the first meeting of the Lincoln County Commissioners 1866

The Board of County Commissioners met pursuant to adjournment at Cottonwood Springs Lincoln County Nebraska Territory at 10 Oclock A M Tuesday October 3rd 1866 Present W M Hinman I C Gilman and I A Morrow Commissioners.

It was ordered by the Board that an Election be held at the house of Chas McDonald in Cottonwood Springs Precinct of Lincoln County Nebraska Territory on Tuesday the 9th day of October 1866. for the following Offices One delegate to Congress One Territorial Auditor One Territorial Treasurer One Territorial Librarian One Councilman and one Representative to the Territorial Legislature One Senator and One Representative to the State Legislature. One Member to the 40th Congress of the United States One County Commissioner for the 2nd District One Coroner One Prosecuting Attorney. Three Judges and two Clerks of Election, And that the proper notice be given accordingly.

Ordered by the Board the County Clerk be authorised to procure Suitable Books for the use of the County and also a Seal for the use of the Office of the County Clerk

The Official Bonds of Wm Baker Sheriff I D Fetchie Probate Judge and I P Boyer were approved and filed by the Board On motion the Board adjourned to meet at the same place on Monday at 10 Oclock A M Oct 8th 1866

Chas McDonald
County Clerk

Minutes of the first meeting of the Lincoln County Commissioners 1866

173

This fall was not a peaceful time for the Gilmans. John was somewhere along the railroad tracks with mules, scrapers, oxen, and wagons. Jerry was trying to keep the store near the fort and to get hay cut. He hired Ferry, a laborer, to stay at the outer ranch to prevent its destruction. Jerry could see that road ranching on the Trail would probably not be profitable for much more than another year. The action would be north of the river along the Union Pacific tracks.

Was it prosperity, loneliness, or just getting up courage? Anyway, when Jerry went into Nebraska City in November, he married Martha's pretty little auburn-haired sister, Elizabeth Alice Fitchie. He brought his tiny bride out to Cottonwood Springs for a short time to share the wild life on the frontier.

Her initiation to the life of the trail was memorable. One day in early December, Jerry left Elizabeth to tend the store. It was a beautiful "Indian summer" day that happens once in a while on the prairie. The store had too long been administered by men so she was busily trying to tidy up the place. Much to her surprise and fright, her first customer was a big Indian brave, clad only in a breech cloth and moccasins.

*　　*　　*

On Christmas Day 1866, the telegraph wires carried the bad news of Fetterman's massacre where General Carrington's troops and many civilian employees were trying to build Fort Phil Kearny on Piney Creek, a branch of Powder River. John "Portugee" Philips, an Indian fighter, trapper and scout, had ridden over two hundred miles through a blizzard to bring the bad news to Fort Laramie.

1866 ended but the struggle with Indians had not.

174

Chapter XI

1867
A NEW AGE

As the cold winds continued to blow from the north and the fine snow powdered down layer after layer, ranches around the Fort could dismiss the Indian problem for the time being, and concentrate on keeping their stock alive and finding enough wood for the stoves to keep themselves from freezing.

However, when the weather was moderate, many of the ranchers and their employees found good excuses to cross the Platte River on the ice to visit the rip-roaring new town of North Platte, situated in the triangle just above the forks of the North and South Platte rivers. The town had been laid out by General Dodge himself in November 1866. Peniston ahd Miller had built their store of logs. John Burke moved an old log building from Cottonwood Springs and transformed it into a hotel of sorts. Andreas reported that: "In fact, so rapidly did the town grow that it was but a short time until there were more than three hundred buildings in the town, and during the winter the population increased to more than five thousand. Many of these were gamblers. In fact, by far the greatest number of the population were gamblers and adventurers.

"From November 1866 to July 1867 the town was made infamous by deeds of violence and disorder done by these lawless mass of floating population. For these few months

North Platte was in every sense of the term a frontier town, where some great event brings a mass of rough and hardy men together. The whiskey saloons were constantly crowded. A large number of gamblers naturally came in that they might by their tricks secure the earnings of the railroad laborers and of the travelers who would visit the town. Drunken brawls were of daily occurrence and vice reigned supreme. The better element was powerless to enforce law and order. Murder and robbery were frequent occurrence. Some of these deeds of violence were punished in the summary manner common to a town where there is no protection from the law. On one occasion the jewelry store of J. M. Lucus, who is yet doing business in North Platte (Note: this was written in 1882) and who for several years treasurer of the county, was broken into by thieves and robbed; but the thieves were pursued—two of them captured and hanged, and the other shot and wounded so badly that his dead body was found some days later."

The buildings were mostly logs or rough boards. Some were tents. One account said that a large tent accommodated gambling devices of all kinds, and a saloon. Boarding places were few and crowded. Some of the railroad workers slept in the crowded bunk cars, or in the shops and the roundhouse, even on carpenter's work benches.

In July when the "end of track" was moved to Julesburg, the population of North Platte diminished to some three hundred.

Rancher John Burke had received the contract for transporting supplies from the end of the railroad at North Platte to Fort McPherson, so contact with the eastern part of the territory continued. The occasional newspaper was read and passed around to neighbors. The editors were busily discussing the pro and con of the pending impeachment of President Johnson. Some were predicting chaos in the country if the Black Man were given the right to vote.

In January, William Bischof, the veteran rancher west of Jack Morrow, had made a trip back to Nebraska City for supplies. While he was gone, he had entrusted his establishment to one of his hands. On his return he found the man so entrusted had gone, taking some $1,200 worth of greenbacks with him!

As usual, John Gilman tried to be at the right place at the right time. West from North Platte, the cedar-filled canyons disappeared. The next wooded areas were south from the Laramie hills. Contractors for wood and ties and trading posts for supplies would have the inside track for profits. But to make money, the contractors had to have capital. It would be interesting to know just when the plans for the Gilmans to team up with the great freighting company of Coe and Carter were made. Did the following circumstances influence the decision?

The Nebraska City *News* reported that late in January Levi Carter bought $10,000 worth of groceries and dry goods in Nebraska City, freighted them to Omaha, shipped them to the end of the track (North Platte), then hauled them to Fort Phil Kearny.

John Bratt wrote later that Coe and Carter lost many wagons and much stock trying to supply hay and wood for the new fort on Piney Wood in late December 1866. Part of the remaining wagons were sent back to Fort Laramie loaded with buffalo hides, elk, deer and other skins, along with bales of furs. The trains pulled by horses and mules went on back to the Missouri River. The ox teams and empty wagons followed to Fort Mitchell, fifty-four miles east of Laramie.

Bratt also reported that Coe and Carter had a store at Fort Mitchell which they sold to a Captain Childs and Jack Sibson partly on time. Sibson had bought out Childs' interest but had not paid Coe and Carter what he owed them.

Bratt said that sometime after he had arrived at Fort Mitchell, the Indians had driven off twenty-eight four-mule teams belonging to John Gilman and Kountz while their train was camped within a quarter of a mile from the Sibson ranch. Mules were expensive!

So it appears that the Gilmans and Coe and Carter needed each other if they were to undertake a large contract that would enable them to reclaim their losses and make a profit. Sometime then during the early part of 1867, the new firm of Gilman and Carter made contractual agreements with officials of the Union Pacific for wood and ties for the Union Pacific west into Wyoming.

NEBRASKA ENTERS THE UNION

Since President Johnson had "pocket vetoed" Nebraska's admission to the Union in 1866, the Nebraska representatives were "knocking at the door" when Congress reassembled in December that same year. Finally, on February 8, 1867 the bill passed, with an amendment restricting Nebraska's right to deny the franchise to men other than "white males" (a part of the state constitution) except Indians. The bill was promptly vetoed by the President on the grounds that the bill did not embrace conditions contained in the enabling act, and the population was too small, but both houses of Congress voted to pass it over his veto.

When the President finally issued the proclamation on March 1, 1867, Nebraska became a state, and another star was added to the flag. The news came west by telegraph and by newspaper, but caused little excitement along the Trail. Washington, D.C. was a world away, and there were too many immediate problems to solve here on the prairie.

CARRINGTON RETURNS

On March 4, Colonel Carrington, now under investigation for the Fetterman massacre, arrived back at Fort McPherson. He was to assume command here, replacing Lieutenant Colonel J K. Mizner. It had been a sad journey, beginning back in late January. The Colonel was accompanied by two companies of the 18th U.S. Infantry and four companies of cavalry. Mrs. Carrington and Widow Drummond and other wives rode in ambulances. The body of Lieutenant Drummond was also brought for burial back at his home. Gray Eagle, Carrington's beautiful thoroughbred horse, given to him by the city of Indianapolis, died from eating tree bark. The Colonel himself was suffering from a serious wound caused by an accident. He had to face not only the problems of a new command but also a board of inquiry concerning the tragedy at Fort Phil Kearny. No doubt this was a severe test of a commander's pride. It was almost a miracle that there were no deaths from frostbite, short rations, snow, and cold on the long trip from Fort Phil Kearny.

The traffic on the old Trail was not as heavy as it had been before the Union Pacific had reached North Platte, but there were still wagons on the Trail. Large outfits, mostly mule teams, were coming through in March. Jim Moore and his brother passed the outer ranch with their twelve wagons, with six mules to a wagon, loaded with merchandise for their ranch beyond Cottonwood Springs. Jerome Dauchy bought Fred White's mule outfit and headed for Julesburg to fulfill a contract with Union Pacific. Billy Campbell and his brother John were preparing to leave Nebraska City for Salt Lake City with twelve four-mule teams and wagons.

By April, everyone along the Platte River was threatened by floods. On April 22 about two miles of the new railroad tracks were washed out, north of the river opposite Dan Smith's ranch. A late spring blizzard halted freighting to Denver for a time. And John Burke, who had worked so hard to build a bridge across the Platte to move his wagons easily from North Platte to Fort McPherson, saw the debris of his bridge scattered along the banks of the rampaging river!

This bridge had been an example of "do-it-yourself" engineering. Anyone who tried to cross the Platte over Burke's bridge must have wondered which was the more dangerous, the quicksand of the Platte or Burke's bridge.

According to Mrs. Maude Hershey's account in the W.P.A. Writer's Program *Sioux Look-Out Country* (1942) the bridge was constructed by placing heavy logs running endwise across the river on top of piles driven into the sand. Then other logs were laid crosswise. The length of the logs were unmatched. Some were from six to eight feet while others were so short that there was scarcely a foot on each side of the wagon track. Brush and slough grass covered the logs. The bridge had no sides and was anchored with old government wagons, weighted down. For the entire time it took to cross the half-mile bridge drivers cursed or cajoled their frightened horses as the heavy wagons jerked and swayed over the serpentine expanse of logs and brush.

Johnny McBride took the Gilman's buggy up to the blacksmith at McDonald's for repairs. Lizzie hadn't been feeling well, so he took her to Nebraska City, joining a large train going east. Fortunately she went when she did, for she was desperately ill in May, and Doctor Larsh sent a telegram to Jerry. Both Jerry and her brother Sam hurried to be with her.

While the men were in Nebraska City, cigar-smokers in lobbies of the local hotels were discussing politics. Democrats were still smarting from the raw deal J. Sterling Morton had received in the 1866 election. He had been nominated as the first governor for the new state, being opposed by David Butler of Pawnee City, the Republican. There were supposed irregularities in the Rock Bluffs, Cass County, election, and consequently, 160 votes were thrown out. This gave Butler the lead, and the Republicans a majority in the legislature.

Nebraska City was also buzzing with speculation concerning the site for the new state capital. Governor David Butler, T. P. Kennard and State Auditor John Gillispie were designated as the committee to decide on a site. Periodically, since the territory had been organized, politicians south of the river had been agitating for a site nearer the center of population.

There was still much rivalry among the river towns. Many resented the fact that Omaha had the territorial capital as well as the eastern terminus of the Union Pacific. Omaha of course wished to keep the capital. A trick attributed to Senator Patrick of Omaha was his insistence that the new capital, south of the river, must be named Lincoln. Assuming that no good Democrat would vote to have the new capital named for a president who had given the railroad terminus to Omaha, he could thus force the capital to be left at Omaha.

But this good Irish trick did not work, for the bill which provided for the selection of the new site, approved on June 14, specifically stated that the commission was to choose a section of land in the south half of Saunders or Butler County, the County of Seward, or the northern part of Lancaster County.

The commission decided upon a small village in Lancaster County. The reasons given were that its location was such that it could be a railroad center, and it was situated near a great salt basin which eventually would be a source of potential wealth. As Jerry listened and smoked his pipe, he would have been surprised if someone had told him that he would spend his last years in the vicinity of the new capital.

The conversations were not all political. The railroad fever had infected the businessmen almost as much as the gold fever of a few years before. Nebraska City merchants did not consider kindly the possibility of having to transport their merchandise to Omaha in order to ship it westward!

After a few days in Nebraska City and when Lizzie was better, Jerry hurried back to the ranch. Sam Fitchie took a subcontract to get out ties for Gilman and Carter in the Lawrence Fork area near Scottsbluff.

As early as June 2, the Indians began their sudden attacks along the Trail. A stagecoach was attacked west of Julesburg. By early August news flashed along the line that a train had been attacked at Plum Creek. Fort Phil Kearny was surrounded, and on August 19, another massacre took place on the Little Blue River. On August 14 the telegraph lines were destroyed between Laramie and Salt Lake City.

By the time Sam Fitchie had finished his contract and had moved on to the new area called Cheyenne City, the army had difficulty in supplying all the troops required to guard the building activities of the railroad and other

181

demands for guard and patrol duties. Many of the small freighting outfits were pressed into government service, so Sam's outfit became government property. About this time Sam contracted the dysentery prevalent around the congested camps, which were not famous for their sanitation. As soon as he was able to travel he hitched a ride back to Nebraska City.

His parents and his sisters were eager to hear all the news he had to tell. He described what he had been told about the new tabernacle which the Mormons had just completed in Salt Lake City. This new building with a semi-egg-shaped roof was held together by green rawhide strips and wooden pegs. This was one way to build without the precious nails which had to be hauled from the Missouri River or from the west coast.

He also told of the happenings around Fort McPherson when he stopped there. The John Burke's had lost their ranch buildings seven miles west of the Fort, and all their stock had been driven away by a thieving band of Sioux, so they had moved in to the Fitchie ranch-house. (This ranch about two miles west of the Fort was later purchased by the Burkes and became their home.)

Things were slow around the ranches. Jerry made a contract with the Fort to furnish 700 cords of wood at $7.90 a cord on July 25. (John Burke and Jacob Snell also had contracts.) Since they had not used all the wood from the previous year, it was soon filled.

Haying had been particularly hazardous. This year they did not go far to the east to cut the hay on Gilman "bottoms" but stayed near the Fort and harvested the hay on one of the islands in the Platte River. Nelson described how the Indians would get into the tall grass and shoot at the workers. Finally Nelson rode in front of the mowing machine with a double-barreled shotgun and wearing his six-shooters. He wrote:

> One day I jumped off my horse to have a skirmish with some of them who were having a lot of fun at my expense. When, as I fired my horse took fright and

bolted. I felt so mad at his leaving me in a lurch, that I faced about and sent a bullet through his head, which effectively prevented his playing me any more of those tricks again. The Gilmans behaved very badly over this. They made me pay for the horse!" (No one abused man or beasts before the Gilmans if they could prevent it!)

Jerry settled his bill with McDonald for his blacksmithing ($209.50) when they were putting up hay, paid off his men, hired A. Rice to guard the outer ranch and went back to Nebraska City. In September he registered as a voter.

Jerry began to enjoy life in civilized society. He became interested in land that was being offered for sale. He enjoyed all the fun in the Fitchie family gatherings, and on November 12, greeted his first-born son, little Frank. Although the boy did not live long, his coming made Jerry decide that he had had enough Indians, wood-chopping and lawlessness. At any rate, John had practically all of their money, stock and equipment tied up with Coe and Carter in Wyoming.

SOMEWHERE IN OLD WYOMING

By the time Jerry had settled back for the winter in Nebraska City, the Union Pacific tracks had passed Pine Bluffs, Wyoming Territory, some seventy-five miles west of Fort Mitchell. Gilman and Carter had a camp at Pine Bluffs, and now moved on to Fort Sanders, which was about two and one-half miles northeast of Laramie. Here quaking aspens grew in abundance and wood was easy to secure. While they were operating this camp they also opened up a camp north of Sherman Station to be headquarters for not only firewood, but ties and telegraph poles. Several hundred men were employed. Many were French-Canadians, skilled in logging, lured by big wages. Others were restless men from the States who had drifted for one reason or another to these centers of work and excitement.

We are indebted to John Bratt for the information about these camps. In his *Trails of Yesterday* he describes his association with the company as their clerk. Bratt had worked for Coe and Carter first at Sibson's ranch, later as a teamster at Fort Phil Kearny, and was one of the fortunate civilians who left with the wagon trains headed back to Laramie just before the Fetterman massacre. In the middle of September he joined the Gilman-Carter camp at Pine Bluffs, where he was hired as a clerk.

The management of these gangs of workers was not easy. Workmen were usually hired by the day or the month and might quit at any time for no reason at all. Bratt tells about a feud between the old employees of the two companies. Those who had worked for Gilmans for many years opposed the "pets" of Coe and Carter. When Bratt assumed the clerkship at Fort Sanders camp, he proposed that both companies get rid of their older pets. Bratt also insisted that there be no whiskey sold at the store. This decision was a terrible blow to the old soaks who were accustomed to helping themselves to the whiskey supply without paying. The feud dissolved when General Coe went to Texas to bring up a herd of cattle and took Bob Mason, John Knox and Matt Brooks with him. Gilman accommodated by sending Gladdon, Hugh Alley, Sharp, Rowland and some others to other jobs. Rowland must have gone back to Nebraska City with a supply train, for he appeared as a registered voter in September 1867.

Like so many of these early ventures, this enterprise was a gigantic game of chance. You gambled on being able to feed and protect your large crew of workmen from the elements, from Indians, and from each other; you gambled on subcontracting to small operators which was necessary if you delivered wood on schedule. Most of these contractors were honest but there was always a few that found it easy to "crib." Wood was sold by the cord. A cord was 8' long, 4' high and 4' wide. The wood was piled in ricks and it was simple to measure the ricks and determine the amount of wood in the piles. But if one cribbed, the rick was hollow or the center loosley piled so the outside dimension would not be an accurate measure of the contents. There were other constant hazards. Teams and wagons were lost when they tried to cross treacherous streams of water. The weather in this region was unpredictable. Bratt tells of riding John Gilman's Kentucky thoroughbred, Oak Rail, on a scouting mission to see if they could cut two thousand tons of hay for the army at Fort Sanders. He was caught in a thunderstorm in which lightning played around both horse and rider and threatened the lives of both. Hard windstorms and sudden blizzards took toll of both men and animals. The Ute Indians raided the herds and drove off horses and cattle. And then there was always fire! One bad fire at Sherman Station burned thirty thousand cords of wood. So the ties which the company bought for thirty-five cents and sold for one dollar delivered to the railroad stations, and the wood that cost from $6.00 to $8.00 and sold for $12.00 to $16.00 was not clear profit!

Paying the subcontractors and men required ingenuity to outwit thieves. The banks nearest to Tie Siding and Sherman Station were in Cheyenne. Clerks or couriers carrying money were attacked by ex-employees who recognized them or by the professional highwaymen who spotted those who carried large sums of money. Once Bratt took elaborate precautions to have one of Ben Gallager's clerks take his horse outside of town for him to cover his departure. He had scarcely mounted when a man sprang out of the dark and grabbed for his bridle rein, but fortunately he escaped.

Money for operation has always been a problem, and the building of the railroad was no exception, All contractors who did business with the railroad ran tremendous risks.

The history of railroad building from the 1830's is a story of heated debates in Congress, squabbles over the proper route for a transcontinental line even after government surveys had been made, and of course there was always the problem of money in fantastic amounts needed to construct the project. Congressmen were wary of federal support, but only the federal government could underwrite this contract. A railroad could not promise a profit for at least ten years after its completion so investors were not interested in taking a chance.

When the railroad act passed Congress in 1862, it provided that the government would grant ten sections of land from the public domain for each mile of railroad built. (Alternate sections on each side of the track) In addition, the government would loan government bonds at the rate of $16,000 per mile of level ground, $32,000 per mile for foothills and $48,000 a mile for mountainous areas. A company was formed and stock was offered for sale, but private investors were not interested.

So later the amount of land was doubled and mortgages for the government bond loaned were liberalized. But not until a stock company controlled by the Union Pacific, promoters called Credit Mobilier of America, became the construction company for the railroad did the tracks begin. The activities of this company were later questioned and a scandal was suspected. Oakes Ames, the manager of Credit Mobilier, also a Congressman from Massachusetts, was said to have distributed stock in the company to members of Congress and public officials below market price and in some cases even loaned them money to buy the stock. He and his brother staked their profitable tool and shovel business on the venture. General Dodge later defended Ames and declared that he was unfairly criticized.

Because Wall Street brokers considered the building of the Union Pacific a wild undertaking, the stocks and bonds did not readily sell on the market. This meant that the Credit Mobilier was often short of ready cash and had to resort to issuing script (negotiable warrants.)

Bratt said that Gilman and Carter were more fortunate than most companies in collecting from Credit Mobilier. Once they were paying out daily five thousand to ten thousand good "greenbacks" and receiving Credit Mobilier script in payment. They sent $1,100,000 in script to bankers in Omaha who would not accept it. But General Coe went to Washington, and after an interview with Thomas Durant, the president of the railroad, he was able to cash part of their claim. Bratt also stated that Gilman and Carter collected over three million dollars for work contracts and did not lose a dollar.

Sprague and Davis Company, who had a tie and wood camp near Tie Siding, were not so fortunate. Some of the tie choppers threatened to hang all the members of the firm because they could not get their pay. Taking them seriously, the firm disappeared one night, leaving the irate choppers unpaid.

It was not easy to keep good workers. The very restlessness which influenced them to come to the territories often took them to other ventures without concern or delay. Men who worked for Gilmans soon developed a loyalty which often brought them back again. Perhaps it was because they were always certain to be paid, given more wages if they were trustworthy and were well fed, or was it the fun which always seemed to be about the Gilman camps? No one loved a good joke better than John K. Gilman.

Bratt gives an example of a practical joke which John played when a well was being dug at the new Union Pacific Hotel in Laramie. While the workers were at dinner, John scattered about twenty dollars' worth of gold dust in the eighteen to twenty-foot-deep well. People gathered around to see the first bucket of water come up. Here was some free gold, and soon a panning operating was under way. In a short time, claims were staked out, and a gold rush began. Fights broke out, one man was killed and several were injured. This joke had backfired. John finally revealed the hoax and restored order by paying for the coffin and setting up drinks and cigars for all those who had been deceived.

When 1867 ended the construction was approaching one of the biggest challenges in bridge building, the Dale Creek Bridge. It was to measure 700 feet long, towering 126 feet high above a small stream bed and secured by ropes and wires against the strong winds and rolling trains. And another chapter would be written "somewhere in old Wyoming."

Chapter XII

1868
THE LAST ROUND-UP

Jerry came back to the ranch as soon as the weather would permit. John had made several hurried trips back from Wyoming, riding on his pass as far as Omaha, then catching a ride down to Nebraska City. The family hoped that John knew what he was doing by investing all they had, except the stock still at the ranch at the Fort and what haying equipment they still had there.

John Nelson describes the activity after Jerry had returned to the Trail. "After I had deen discharged from the hospital I hung about the Fort for a few weeks until I felt thoroughly set up. Then I went to the Gilmans to see what they could do for me. The soldiers had returned from the outside ranche, and, as there was no one left to look after it, I was asked if I would. A fair amount of stock had been taken out there in anticipation of the Indians being driven right away from the road, but it seemed an almost hopeless task on the part of the military to drive them away. It was arranged that I should go out with my wife and the children and remain three months. At the expiration of that time the commandant thought he would be able to drive the Indians out into the prairie and keep them there.

"We packed up our traps and went out under guard. The soldiers left us, only returning every now and then when they wanted anything.

"I took possession of the fort, which was about forty steps away from the ranch, and consisted of a circular room some twelve feet in diameter, excavated in the ground, with an underground passage from it running to the stables. A stockade surrounded it, absolutely impregnable, at least from attacks by Indians.

"I had not been there very long before I had some visits from my red friends, who would creep up and try to carry the place by stealth.

"I had a thousand rounds of ammunition, and my wife loaded my rifles whilst I blazed away. I killed several Indians and their horses whilst I was there.

"Over and over again I have killed antelopes through the chinks in the stockade, and run out to fetch them in.

"One of my chief amusements was to ride out into the prairie and draw the Indians after me, then run into my hole and open fire on them.

"After a time they would not come near me, but ride round in a circle of which I was the center, at about one thousand yards' range, and whoop, and yell, hoping to draw me out. But I never nibbled at that bait.

"Finally, the Gilmans determined, as the ranche cost them more to keep up than it brought in, to pull it down, especially as, wood being scarce, they received a good offer from the railway people for it. Accordingly a party of men came out from the siding under military escort with a lot of wagons, and demolished and carried it into the Fort with all the remaining stock.

"My wife and I took our departure at the same time, and when I returned I found myself looked upon as a sort of hero for having held out as long as I had."

Jerry stayed at the branch establishment at the Fort, caring for the stock they still had there and getting the four mowers and other equipment repaired before it was time to hay. (Nelson said that the Gilmans were the hay contractors for the Fort.)

One day when Jerry went down to the post office for the mail, he met a newcomer. It was Wild Bill Hickok, who had shown up at the Fort and stayed for a short time, scouting for troops and killing buffalo.

Attempts were being made to make peace with the Indians. In September of 1867 runners were sent throughout the Sioux country, inviting the chiefs to assemble again at Laramie. But there seemed to be little interest. Red Cloud insisted that councils were useless as long as the white man continued to violate the past treaty by traveling the Bozeman Trail. When the army withdrew troops from Fort C. F. Smith and from Fort Phil Kearny, in April 1868 Red Cloud came in. The Sioux agreed to stay in an area north of Nebraska and west of the Missouri River (land which they had always claimed) if allowed to hunt in areas where they had always hunted. They also agreed to allow the railroad and some other roads to be built through their territory.

As Nelson had stated, this did not settle the problem. Crazy Horse, Sitting Bull and northern Cheyenne continued to go where they pleased. Attempts to keep Indians on given reservations continued for many years. Unfortunate incidents continued to be perpetrated by Whites, especially after it was known that gold had been discovered in the Black Hills, the sacred mountains of the Sioux.

The soldiers were kept busy guarding the railroad; and watching for hit and run attacks. On September 18, Colonel Forsyth and fifty scouts held out against Chief Roman Nose and several hundred Indians at the famous battle of Beechers Island. On September 24, 1868 a large gathering of Sioux, Cheyenne and Pawnee Indians met in council with General Sherman, General Harvey and John P. Sanborne. This council was held in the new railroad roundhouse in North Platte.

Soon after the end-of-track activities were moved to Julesburg, North Platte settled down to becoming a real village. The gambling shacks and saloons, the girlie entertainers, and the drifters had all departed like vultures to feed upon the victims on the U. P. payroll. Frame houses began to take the place of log cabins. Machine shops beside the new roundhouse identified North Platte as a division

190

headquarters of the railroad. At the election held in the fall of 1867, it was decided to move the county seat from Cottonwood Springs to North Platte, so this was done officially November 12. There was no courthouse at that time. The commissioners met in W. M. Hinman's log house, and each officer kept his books in his own home. (It is surprising that we are still able to read the old commissioner's proceedings.)

Fulfilling the hay contract this year was very difficult. Herman Angell decided to try his luck again, and came out to help hay. He and his crew were attacked, and again he was the only one to survive. Altogether, seven men were killed in the vicinity of the Fort.

After the hay had been delivered, Jerry sold off the remaining stock and the few supplies at the branch establishment, all except enough wagons and stock needed to farm the land near Nebraska City. It was with mixed emotions that the little outfit left Cottonwood Springs. John Nelson left his family with his wife's relatives and went with Jerry. Johnny McBride drove the stock. They joined an escorted train that had come in from the west. They shook hands with all the old friends around the Fort and the little settlement at Cottonwood Springs—some they would never see again.

There must have been many memories as they headed east for the last time. The wagons moved so slowly that there was time to remember the dances at McDonalds, the time the army commandant had shut up Boyer's bar and confiscated his supply of whiskey, the buffalo hunts and the narrow escapes. On past Snells, past Machette's ranch, which would survive long after the other buildings along the Trail had disappeared, the stage station where Trout had last served the stage line. Twelve miles farther they camped at the old campground just beyond the outer ranch site.

The stripped ranch site that had been home for eight years looked as if it had been massacred. Only the stage station and the soddies remained of the once busy ranch which had required so many hours of hard work. There had been a prairie fire in July and the gaunt blackened

191

telegraph poles stood like ghostly trail markers. But the iron pump remained. Although the red paint had blistered in the hot sun and creeping fire, and it had rusted to a bronze, it still gave forth cold clear water. At the well north of the Trail near the place where the post had been, the curbing was blackened and the rope had burned away.

After the wagon train had camped for the night, the three men walked back to the site. Picking up an empty bottle and a mule shoe, and examining the pit where Nelson had buried the carcasses of the animals that he had killed and skinned for their hide, each was remembering. The ghost of Two Face seemed very near. They reminded each other of the post where the express pony had been tied; the posts used to mark the distance when horses were raced for sport. Part of one soddy had already fallen in where the cedar ridgepole had been burned. In a very short time, the prairie would cover the spot just as it had the graves along the Trail and other habitations in the past.

Early the next morning the wagon train stretched out along the Trail, and the military guard assumed their vigil. There were shadows far across the bronzed-grass Platte Valley marking the canyon where so many cedars had been felled and hauled. The canyon was the only signature that the Gilmans left to mark the spot where they had labored. (Only on old soils maps of Lincoln County do you find the Gilman name designating that canyon where they had left the mark of their axes on the stump of cedar trees.) They passed the old Indian campground, now deserted, where they had first traded with the Indians.

The train halted for the night near Dan Smith's west ranch. Here again they solemnly said farewell to this neighbor who had shared many of their experiences. Dan Smith was a strange man. No one knew what he was thinking. Those who had worked with him knew that his was a jealous nature, and his temper could be quick and deadly, but he was a hard worker and that was an admirable quality.

The next days were monotonous and uneventful. Past Cold Water ranch, now almost deserted since Miller and

Peniston had moved to North Platte. The remains of their burned-out ranch squatted in the tall grass. The valley was still dotted with bleaching bison bones and broken wagons and trash around the camping grounds. They camped near the site of Freeman's old ranch, now rebuilt across the valley beside the railroad. The cluster of graves from the Plum Creek massacre was pointed out by old-timers to those of the train who had not traveled this way before. Nelson called attention to a spot near the river where Bill Cody had killed his first Indian back in the '50's.

As they approached Dobytown, they could see the flag flying over Fort Kearny two miles down the road. It was a welcome sign, for it meant that they were now approaching civilization. John Nelson entertained Johnny McBride by telling him of the short time that he had operated a saloon in Dobytown.

On and on through the late summer's heat. More and more travelers seemed to be on the road. Little farm houses surrounded by cultivated fields lined the road sides.

On October 17, 1868 Jerry bought the Judge Reed quarter west of Nebraska City. He and John bought more land in this vicinity. Jerry's house was on the Old Steam Wagon Road just west of J. Sterling Morton's home place. John Nelson stayed with them until they were well established in their new home. He dismisses the Gilmans in his book by saying: "During the seven years that they had been trading—I had been with them the whole time off and on—they had made over two hundred thousand dollars. I had materially aided in this, but I was not invited to participate in the division of the plunder."

The decade from 1859-1869 was almost completed. The old freighters, the stage drivers, loggers and Pony Express riders would tell and retell the legends of the Trail in the years to come. Some would lie a little to make the story better, some would ascribe the experiences of others to themselves and tell them so often that they would believe them, some would get the facts a little confused as memories began to dim. Heroes would be made from commonplace men by pens of the magazine writers, real heroes would be forgotten. The tide of settlement moved on. Cattle would move about the lush Platte Valley, and later ranchers would move in and plant trees for their tree claims. Only the rusty pump on the prairie extended its iron skyward as a symbol of the courage, fortitude, hospitality and integrity that existed when a nation was tied together by thin wires on cedar poles, and rolling wheels powered by plodding oxen or pounding hoofs.

POSTLUDE

After 1868

For the next two or three years fewer and fewer wagons traveled south of the river. Grass began to creep into the ruts of the Trail, and fire continued to blot out old landmarks. In 1869 Ericssons homesteaded near the Fort, at the mouth of Snell Canyon. By 1871 the county of Lincoln had been completely surveyed. The western portion of old Shorter County became Cheyenne County in 1870.

Gilman and Carter continued to supply the railroad until the golden spike was driven in 1869. Gilman and Carter, merchants and contractors, were listed in the history of Albany County, Wyoming Territory, as having one of the leading business establishments in Sherman in 1869.

Coe and Carter also went into the cattle business, driving cattle from Texas and fattening them on western ranches. After the contract with Union Pacific had terminated, they brought their outfits to the Fort McPherson area to fill a big contract for government hay. When this was accomplished, the company dissolved partnership and liquidated their assets. Bratt stated that the company cleared about a million dollars in their railroad contracts.

Fort McPherson continued to offer protection to the railroad and to those traveling west, keeping a watchful eye on the Indians. The fort now took on a new role. It became a base for the entertainment of V.I.P.'s who came to hunt buffalo. Many parties of politicians, railroad officials and even foreigners were treated to spectacular hunting expeditions. Here Bill Cody, who had come as a scout with General E. A. Carr, added to his legend for shooting. He had won his title of Buffalo Bill while acting as official hunter for the Kansas Pacific Railroad when it was under construction.

The fort was abandoned and the buildings were sold at auction in 1880. (Some of the buildings are still in existence.) Only a monument remains to mark the spot where the flagpole once stood. The beautiful valley is now under cultivation. An irrigation canal furnishes irrigation water for the rich black soil.

After the partnership was dissolved, John Gilman joined his family in Nebraska City. (Mat had remained in the city after she had almost been killed by Indians in 1865 when her brother Sam, little George and she had been surrounded by some three hundred savages.)

But John was not content to enjoy the wealth earned in the last ten years. The phantom of adventure now was a four letter word—g-o-l-d! He had invested in some claims in North Park, Colorado while they were still in Wyoming. But later with S. F. Nuckolls, a prominent Nebraska City merchant and politician, he went to prospect in the Watsash Mountains near Salt Lake City. They lost heavily. Nuckolls remained in Wyoming and served the new state.

When the gold fields were opened in the Black Hills, John in partnership with Robert Hawke, the richest man in Otoe County, went to buy claims near Deadwood. Here he spent the rest of his life and all the Gilman fortune seeking gold. It was said that they had valuable claims in or near the heart of the quartz region but lost them through litigation. Legal battles were prevalent. The government had rescinded early claim rights. Claim jumping was a common practice. John died in 1887. His obituary stated that he had won his court case in South Dakota in the summer of 1886. About that time a new silver mining company was

Jeremiah Gilman in later life

organized and registered in Deadwood. John Gilman was the president. But his health and fine fortune were gone. All their business dealings had always been in a joint account.

Jerry was able to salvage part of the land and continued to live on his Nebraska City farm until 1898. In the book, *Portrait and Biographical Album of Otoe County* by Chapman Brothers, published March 1889, his biography ends:

> Though past the prime of life, he is active and enterprising as many a younger man, and is always busy looking after his agricultural interests, and carefully manages his property so as to get the best returns from it. He possesses a clear head and a sound intellect, and is a man to be relied upon in any and every case. He is a sturdy advocate of the policy of the Republican party, and is keenly interested in all the questions of the day that pertain to the welfare of our country. (The Gilmans moved to Lancaster County near Lincoln in 1898, and Jerry died in 1904.)

John Gilman had four children—George, Dollie, Minnie and John K., Jr. Jeremiah had eight children—Frank and Pike (who died in infancy), Larsh, Andrew, Nellie, Duke, Lee and Charles.

Billy Campbell, the pony express rider, married his Jennie Fitchie, bought land near Nebraska City and improved it. While living in eastern Nebraska, he served in the legislature. Since he was one of the last living Pony Express riders, he supplied many of the details of the history in later years. He moved to California and amassed a fortune breeding horses.

Charles McDonald remained at Cottonwood Springs until 1872, when he moved to North Platte to become an important businessman there. The McDonald bank which he established is still in existence.

Jerome Dauchy, the hotelkeeper at Gilmans in 1860, had a road ranch of his own for a time; spent some time in Denver; freighted and eventually became a citizen of Frontier County. He served as a county commissioner and as county treasurer. He died in 1897.

Henry Clifford had been with the Gilmans from the beginning of their ranching activities. It is thought that his younger brother, Mortimer, or Monte, as he was called, also worked for them. They had also worked for Jerome Dauchy. Frontier County was organized in Henry's lodge.

Henry had married Maggie, a Cheyenne Indian girl. Monte married Julia, a Sioux, related to Spotted Tail. Her father was Augustine Lutice, a French trapper. He had been an interpreter and a scout for Lieutenant Grattan. He was killed in the Grattan massacre.

The Cliffords settled on Medicine Creek, south of Fort McPherson, living in tepees as their Indian relatives did. John Bratt describes the hilarious occasion when the cattlemen in the area met in Henry's lodge to organize the county on January 5, 1872. No one had a pen to sign the document so an old steel pen was tied to a dry weed and soot was used for ink. Our old friend, John Nelson, was elected county surveyor, although he knew nothing about surveying.

Henry operated a store for a time, later did business off and on the Indian reservation. In 1900 he and John Nelson were employed as guides through the Badlands. He died at Pine Ridge in 1906.

Monte lost his Frontier County land to McDonald's store in payment of a large store bill. His wife's relatives literally ate him out of house and home. He lived for a time in Stockville, then took his six children to the reservation. He died in 1904 near Martin, South Dakota.

Perhaps one of the most dramatic stories of the ranchers was that of Dan Smith, who had first built Cold Water ranch east of Midway Stage Station, then a west ranch about five miles east of Midway. Local legend has it, that he and his wife were still living at the west ranch in 1871. Mrs. Smith wished to attend a ball at Fort McPherson. Dan, who was insanely jealous of her, would not allow her to go with neighbors. They quarreled. Mrs. Smith was determined to go. She saddled her horse and started to leave alone. Dan called to her, suggesting that she come back and take a gun to protect her from Indians. She turned. He fired, killing her instantly. The local ending said that Dan rode off into the canyon, and the soldiers hunted him down and killed him. But in 1874, Dan Smith, the old plainsman, who had "accidently" killed his wife some years before, had murdered a man named Ross, at Dale Creek, according to the Cheyenne Sentinal. The paper stated that Dan had probably fled south.

Pat Mullally (whose name was probably mispelled more times than any other) had been at Willow Island as far back as June 1860 when the census was taken. His ranch usually bore his name or that of Willow Island. He had had a partner House or Housel. Old R. C. Freeman had been there for a long time also. Their first cabin was probably one for trappers. When troops were stationed there in 1864-65 the place was called Fort Willow Island.

Pat, like many of the ranchers, would disappear at intervals, sometimes going back to the States, other times going west to the mines or at rails-end where the excitement was. Sometime in the late 1866, he left his ranch in charge of Freeman. No one at the ranch saw or heard from him.

Years later, however, in the history of Wyoming, an account was given concerning the first city election in the new town of Cheyenne on September 7, 1867. A Pat Mullally was one of the members of a fifty-eight man police force which had been organized when General Dodge laid out the city.

Mullally had built a two-story frame building and opened a saloon. He did a thriving business, and made many friends in the new city.

According to the newspaper account, some bad characters, including one "Limber Jim," began to flock around him, presumably demoralizing him. He quarreled with a rival saloon and resort keeper referred to as "Lead Beader."

On September 16, Pat, Limber Jim and two females went up to Lead Beader's. The door was closed. Limber Jim and Pat proceeded to open it. Pat was shot by someone under the bed. Jim ran but was shot in the back. This caused a riot and the cavalry had to be called out from Fort Russell.

Pat Mullally had a brother, Tom. He first saw Nebraska in 1861. He went on to Pike's Peak and stayed there until 1863. His biography stated that he settled on a ranch about fifty miles west of Fort Kearny. (This was the same area as Willow Island.) He went to Cheyenne in 1867. In 1870 he returned to the area in the Republican Valley, locating on Turkey Creek in Harlan County. Sixteen other men came at the same time. There is a precinct in this county named for Tom.

John Nelson continued to drift back and forth from scouting for the army to living with the Indians. The Reverend John Robinson, a Methodist minister at Fort McPherson, insisted that Nelson marry his squaw. He was then to call her his wife. He and Cliffords conducted several enterprises with the Indians after their sojourn in Frontier County. He tried his luck freighting to the mines in South Dakota. He served for a time as a postmaster on the Sidney-Black Hills route. His great experience came when he and his family traveled with his old friend, Bill Cody and His Wild West Show.

His daughter, Mrs. Joe Ecoffey, wrote in 1933 that Nelson had died on the Pine Ridge Reservation in January 1903 and is buried in the Episcopal cemetery there.

Johnnie McBride appeared on the 1870 census with the Gilmans. The family said that he was killed when a horse fell.

Jack (John Andrew) Morrow, the well-known rancher some twelve miles west of Fort McPherson, was not only a colorful figure but a controversial one as well. He has been pictured by his contemporaries as a thief, a scoundrel, a character most Easterners saw as the typical Westerner. Many travelers mention his diamond shirt stud, and his habit of drinking champagne from a tin cup. Mrs. Carrington, however, described him as a gentleman. He had the reputation for poker playing from Omaha to Denver.

He also furnished ties and timber for the Union Pacific railroad, then left the Trail in 1868. Some say he moved to

Omaha to spend the fortune that he had earned, but others say that the soldiers urged him to leave, for they were tired of looking for stolen horses.

After he left the Trail he still contracted with the Union Pacific and stage companies for supplies. He was a sutler at Fort Abraham Lincoln for a time.

When he died at the age of 45 of consumption or pneumonia, his body was returned to Washington, Pennsylvania for burial. His obituary told that he had married his wife, Jane Wood, some years before he left the Trail. None of the old diaries mentioned a white wife.

John Burke continued to make his home west of Cottonwood Springs. He accumulated a sizable fortune, but lost his life trying to freight across his Platte River bridge when the river was having one of its tantrums.

W. M. Hinman lived out his life in this area. He had a store in North Platte. He later moved to a ranch outside North Platte.

One of the mystery ranchers on the Trail from Fort Kearny to Fort McPherson was Blondeau. Eugene Ware mentioned that they always stopped at Blondeaus on their way. Diaries mentioned that Plum Creek had two stores. Most people took for granted that they were Freemans and Thomas ranches. (Thomas was the postmaster.) But Freemans were not at Plum Creek until 1864.

The Dawson County Historical Society received three old account books written in French. Here was a clue to the mystery. On the census of 1860, Louis Wiscamb (or Wiscamp), trader, was listed just down the Trail from Patrick Mullally's. He had four Frenchmen working for him. The old account books revealed that Bernard Silvoier Blondeau was his partner at Plum Creek, off and on, in 1861, 1863, and 1864. In 1862 he kept a ranch "two miles after Bouvais" which was much farther west. His son, Jules, was also with him.

In the account book was the address of Jules' son, who lives in St. Joseph, Missouri. He proved to be a responsive correspondent. Mr. W. L. Blondeau revealed that his grandfather, B. S. Blondeau's family had been part of a

French company who set out to establish a model community, "Icaria," in the new world. The Blondeau family ended up in St. Joseph. Bernard operated a store at Sugar Creek, Missouri as well as trading with Indians and pilgrims. The family were friends with both the Robideaus and the Bouvais.

So the Plum Creek ranch is no longer a mystery. It was operated by Louis Wiscamb and B. S. Blondeau.

Sam Fitchie sold his house at Box Elder to John Burke in 1867 and went on to Cheyenne. He hauled timber from the Black Hills when Fort Russell was built. He returned to Nebraska City and entered into business there and in Weeping Water. In later years he was active in the Prohibition Party and traveled over the Midwest as a lay minister. He spent his last days in University Place, a suburb of Lincoln.

Many of the young men who spent the decade on the Trail became leading businessmen in their settled communities. Others drifted to the mines in the west, or just dropped out of sight.

We who are privileged to live in the "moon age" are accustomed to spectacular achievements, and it is easy for us to forget that such things as railroads and telegraph lines which we take for granted were once giant steps in the age in which they came.

Perhaps every age has something in common—uncommon men. Men of curiosity and courage, who have faith in themselves, and in the reliability of natural and spiritual laws. Those who break ground for the new age by gambling their future, their fortunes, and their lives against tremendous odds.

LOCATION OF ROAD RANCHES FROM
FORT KEARNY TO JULESBURG, 1859-1866

There has been much discussion concerning the location of old road ranches in the Platte Valley. The area was unsurveyed government land until 1869-71, consequently, the sites were not recorded.

After the railroad came north of the river in 1866, the ranchers moved out of the valley. Most of the area reverted back to prairie where weather, fire and grass erased landmarks. After the Indian threat disappeared, the lush Platte valley sustained large herds of cattle. Finally settlers and their plows changed the valley. Later irrigation projects raised the water table, making excavations very difficult.

Information from old records and diaries do not always agree. Travelers were more often interested in fuel, water supply or campgrounds than in ranches. Mileages often were determined by the season, the number of mud holes that needed to be bypassed, or the amount of traffic at any given time.

The same establishment might be called by several different names. Spelling was not a virtue. Hindman and Hinman referred to the same man. Peniston, Penniston, Penneston was part owner of Cold Water station. Dutch Smith had a ranch near Plum Creek while Dan Smith had interests in two ranches, one on either side of Midway Stage station. There were four Freemans operating on the frontier at the same time, none were related. Mr. Curran, who took the census in 1860, was most careless with given names.

One of the most interesting discussions had to do with the mystery of pony express and stage stations at Cottonwood Springs and Box Elder just two to three miles away. The truth is there was but one station about half way between McDonald's and Box Elder. If you were traveling west you called it Cottonwood Springs; going east you called it Box Elder. (See Sitgreaves map of the environs of Cottonwood Springs.) The Salt Lake Stage station was built by early 1859. McDonald did not buy Dick Darling's building until late 1859, and moved there in Janaury 1860.

Daniel Freeman's ranch near Plum Creek has also provided discussion. Notice the early mileage charts show his ranch some three to five miles west of Plum Creek. Yet Sitgreaves shows the ranch very near to the fort. Both are true. Soon after the Plum Creek massacre, Mrs. Freeman took her children to safety. While they were gone the ranch was burned. Freeman rebuilt near the fort.

Visitors stop at a little cemetery near the Plum Creek ranch site. Here a sign indicates that eleven men from Iowa were masscred here in August 1864. The actual common grave is about 1-1/2 miles east of this place. (Carlyle's testimony, and information from Mr. Clyde Wallace, whose family has lived here for many years.)

The following legal descriptions of the principal ranches were determined from these sources: The original survey maps showing the location of the old wagon road (State Surveyor's office); approximate mileages given by newspapers of the day, old diaries, stage coach schedules; consultation with local citizens who have been interested in the subject. Credit for the location of Willow Island (Mullally's) is given to Mrs. Charles Phillips, Cozad, Nebraska (deceased) from a letter to Mr. A. E. Sheldon, Nebraska Historical Society on January 21, 1937. The location of the sites in Keith County was given by Mr. Pete Peters who has dug these sites for artifacts. Not only the legal description but also the map of the Gilman ranch site

was prepared by Mrs. Lyle Bailey, Gothenburg, Nebraska.
The Baileys are present owners of the site. (The main area is
still in native meadow.)

RANCHES	COUNTY	RANGE	TWP.	SECTION
(Fort Kearny)	Kearney	15W	8N	22
Kearny City (Dobytown)	Kearney	16W	8N	Part of 19-30
Plum Creek	Phelps	20W	8N	Parts of 8 & 9
Willow Island (Mullally's)	Dawson	22W	9N	Lot 1 Sec. 8
Smith's East (Miller & Peniston)	Dawson	23W	10N	19
Midway Stage Station (Approximate)	Dawson	24W	10N	8
Smith's West	Dawson	25W	11N	34
Gilmans	Lincoln	26W	11N	4
Clark's	Lincoln	27W	11N	26 or 27
Machette	Lincoln	28W	12N	14
McDonald's	Lincoln	28W	12N	15
(Fort McPherson)	Lincoln	28W	12N	9
(Reservation survey 1869—sections, 3,4,5,8,9,10,15,16,17)				
Box Elder	Lincoln	29W	12N	27

RANCHES	COUNTY	RANGE	TWP.	SECTION
Jack Morrow	Lincoln	29W	12N	20
Cold Springs	- Lincoln	30W	13N	—18
Bischof (Bishop) (This is an estimate)	Lincoln	31W	13	5
Fremont Springs (Marker)	Lincoln	32W	13N	4

Since the road changed here, these are approximate sites.

O'Fallons Bluff	Lincoln	33W	13N	34
Bob Williams	Lincoln	33W	13N	32
Moore's	Lincoln	33W	13N	6
Elkhorn	Keith	35W	13N	8
Alkali #1	Keith	36W	13N	7
#2	Keith	37W	13N	12
Junction	Keith	38W	13N	2
Sandhill	Keith	38W	13N	8
Diamond Springs	Keith	40W	13N	21
Beauvais	Keith	41W	13N	25

Julesburg, Colorado after 1861. There were four Julesburgs. The first three were south of the South Platte River between the present Julesburg and Ovid.

COMPARATIVE
LIST OF ROAD RANCHES AND MILEAGE
Fort Kearny to Julesburg 1859-1866

Sources: (1) Rocky Mt. News, May 7, 1959 (2) C. M. Clark Spring 1860 (3) Western Stage, Omaha April 1861 (4) McMechan, People's Press, Nebraska City

* 1861 indicates Western Stage Stations

1 1859		2 1860		3 1861		4 1862	
Fort Kearny		Fort Kearny		Fort Kearny		Fort Kearny	
17 Mile Pt.	17	Shakespear	19	Kearny		Dobytown	2
Plum Creek	20	Plum Creek	15	City	2	Stage St.	5
Brady Is.	31	Willow Is.	15	Beerman	1	Keeler	3
Cottonwood							
Springs	6	Smith's	8	Keeler	6	Young	8
Box Elder	3	Stage St.	4	Young	3-1/2	Biddleman	5
Fremont		Gilmans	13	P.E.		Smith's	
Springs	19	Cottonwood		Express	3-1/2	(new)	3
O'Fallons	16	Springs	15	Sydenham	3-1/2	Plum Creek	11
Moore &		J. Morrow	12	Iowa		Parsons	2
Grimes	2	Bishop	12	(Gardiner)	3	Sharp	3
South Platte		Fremont Sl.		Davidson		P. Molair	12
Fork	40	Fremont		(25 mile)	3	D. Smith	E.8
		Springs	8	F. Smith	3	Midway	5
		B. Williams	6	Finley &		D. Smith	W.5
		U.S. Mail	2	Burtch	4	Gilmans	10
		Moore &		Plum Creek	6	Clark	
		Grimes		Stage		McDonald	7
		Pike's Peak	16	Station	1	Mosbatt	3
		Lower		Parson	2	Cottonwood	5
		Crossing	20	J. Sharp	2	J. Morrow	12
		Upper		D. Freeman		Stage	5
		Crossing	22		3	Bishop	7
				Ranch	9	Fremont Sp.	8
				*Smith's	9	O'Fallons	5
				C. Stage	10	Williams	2
				Springville	4	Moore	2
				McDonald		J. Dauchy	2
				Clark	13	Alkali	16
				Capitol		C. Walker	2
				(Machett)		Lone Tree	9
				Cottonwood		Stage St.	7
				Springs		Lower C.	3
				Baldwin &		Bakers	3
				Pegram	2	Michigan	17
				Hays Bro.	1	Julesburg	19
				Hinman	1	1861 continued	
				Junction	2	Williams	8
				*Fremont		Moore	3
				Slough	11	J. Dauchy	2
				Fremont Sp.	9	P.E. Express	25
				O'Fallons	5	Beauvais	3

5 1863		6 1864		7 1865		8 1866	
Fort Kearny		Fort Kearny		Fort Kearny		Fort Kearny	
Platte	10	Gardner's	25	Craig	10	Dobytown	2
Craig	11	French's	25	Platte		Townsend	8
Plum Creek	15	Smith's R.	25	Station	10	McClain &	
Willow Is.	15	Gilmans	? 10	Plum Creek	15	Russell	6
Midway	14	Cottonwood	15	Willow Is.	15	Platte	
Gilmans	15			Midway	10	Stage	8
Cottonwood	17			D. Smith	10	Plum Creek	13
Cold Springs	15			Gilmans	10	Freeman	6
Fremont Sp.	14			D. Trout	12	Mullally's	10
Alkali Lake	14			Post		Miller &	
Sand Hill	12			Cottonwood	4	Penneston	9
Diamond Sp.	11			Box Elder	3	Midway	5
South Platte	15			J. Morrow	10	D. Smith	5
Julesburg	14			Bishops	10	Gilmans	10
Source:		Source:		Fremont Sp.	10	Frost's	14
Root & Connelley		E. Ware		O'Fallons	2	Ft. McPherson	3
Overland Stage				Elkhorn	10	Fitchie's	2
***				Alkali	15	Box Elder	1
Fort Kearny				Sand Hill	10	Morrow	7
Dobytown	2			Diamond		Cold Spr.	5
Platte Station				Springs	10	Bishop's	7
Craig	17			Elbow	10	O'Fallons	
Plum Creek	17			Butte	10	Military	
Willow Is.	15			Julesburg	10	Post	10
Midway	?			Source:		B. Williams	5
Gilmans	15			Geo. O'Brien		Moore	3
Cottonwood	15			7th Cavalry		Elkhorn	
Morrow's	12					Stage	2
Cold Springs	15					Alkali	15
Fremont St.	12					Omaha	5
Elkhorn	?					Sand Hill	5
Rising Sun	2					Diamond Spr.	10
(w. of O'F.)						Beauvais	3
Alkali Lake	14					South Platte	11
Lower Cal.	15					Butt's	6
Julesburg	14					Julesburg	10

Source:
Frank Helvey,
an old freighter

Source:
Army Report on
Ranches 1866
from
Mattes *Great
Platte Valley Road*

210

BIBLIOGRAPHY

From the vast library of special interest books, I have found these to be most helpful:

Andreas, A. T. (Compiler) *History of the State of Nebraska.* Chicago: Western Historical Company, 1882.

Bare, Ira and William McDonald. *History of Lincoln County* (Nebraska). Chicago and New York: American Historical Society, 1920.

Beach, Mrs. Alfred H. *Women of Wyoming.* Casper: S. E. Boyer and Company, 1927.

Bloss, Roy S. *Pony Express—the Great Gamble.* Berkeley, California: Howell-North, 1959.

Bratt, John. *Trails of Yesterday.* Lincoln, Nebraska: University Publishing Company, 1921.

Brown, Dee. *Fort Phil Kearney.* New York: Putnam's Sons, 1962.

Burton, Sir Richard Francis. *The Look of the West, 1860 Across the Plains to California.* London: Longman, Green, Longman, and Roberts, 1862; Reprint from the Second Edition, Lincoln, Nebraska: University Press.

Carrington, Mrs. Frances C. *Army Life on the Plains.* Philadelphia and London, J. P. Lippincott Co. 1910.

Carrington, M. I. *Ab-Sa-Ra-Ka, Home of the Crows.* Philadelphia: J. B. Lippincott and Co. 1868.

Chapman Brothers. *Portrait and Biographical Album of Otoe County* (Nebraska). Chicago. Chapman Brothers, 1889.

Clark, Charles M., M.D. *A Trip to Pike's Peak and Notes by the way.* Chicago: S. P. Rounds Steam Book and Job Printing House, 1861.

Clinkenbeard, Anna Dell. *Across the Plains in '64 by Prairie Schooner to Oregon.* New York, Exposition Press, 1953.

Cody, William F. *Life and Adventures of Buffalo Bill.* New York: Willey Book Co., 1927.

Collins, John S. *Across the Plains in '64.* Omaha: National Printing Company, 1904.

Combs, Barry B. *Westward to Promontory.* Palo Alto, California: American West Publishing Company, 1969.

Compendium of History Reminiscences and Biography. Alden Publishing Company, 1909.

Cook, James H. *Fifty Years on the Old Frontier.* Yale Press, 1923; reprint Norman Oklahoma: University of Oklahoma Press, 1963.

Coutant, C. G. *History of Wyoming.* Laramie: 1899.

Dale, E. E. *Cow Country.* Norman: University of Oklahoma, 1942.

Dale, Raymond E. *Biographical Dictionary of Otoe County* (Nebraska) *Pioneers.* Lincoln, Nebraska: (typed) 1961.

D.A.R. *Nebraska Pioneer Reminiscences.* Cedar Rapids, Iowa: Torch Press, 1916.

Dawson, Charles *Pioneer Tales of the Oregon Trail and Jefferson County.* Topeka: 1912.

Delano, Alonzo. *Life on the Plains and Among the Diggings.* Auburn and Buffalo, 1854.

DeVoto, Bernard. *Across the Wide Missouri.* Boston: Houghton Mifflin, 1947.

Dick, Everett. *Sod-House Frontier.* New York: Appleton-Century Co., 1937.

Dodge, Grenville M. *How We Built the Union Pacific, 1866-70.* Denver: Sage Books (Reprint 1965)

Eggenhofer, Nick. *Wagons, Mules and Men.* New York: Hastings House, 1961.

Frederick, James Vincent. *Ben Holladay, the Stage Coach King.* Glendale: Arthur H. Clark Co., 1940.

Gray, A. A. *Men Who Built the West.* Caxton Printers, 1946.

Greeley, Horace. *Overland Journey, New York to San Francisco.* New York: Saxton, 1860.

Hafen, LeRoy R. *Overland Routes to the Gold Fields from Contemporary Diaries.* Glendale, California: Arthur Clark Co., 1942.

Hafen, LeRoy R. *The Overland Mail 1849-69.* Cleveland: Arthur H. Clark Co., 1926.

Hassrick, Royal B. *The Sioux—Life and Customs of a Warrior Society.* Norman, Oklahoma: University of Oklahoma Press, 1964.

Hebard, Grace Raymond. *History of Wyoming.* San Francisco: C. F. Weber, 1926.

Hirshson, Stanley P. *Grenville M. Dodge.* Bloomington: Indiana University Press, 1967.

Holmes, Louis A. *Fort McPherson Guardian of the Tracks and Trails.* Lincoln, Nebraska: Johnsen Publishing Co., 1963.

Jackson, W. Turrentine. *Wagon Roads West.* Berkeley: University of California Press. 1952.

Jensen, Marion A. *Operation West.* Detroit: Harlo Press, 1962.

Kuykendall, William L. *Frontier Days.* Kuykendall, 1917.

Loveland, Cyrus C. *California Trail Herd.* Talisman Press, 1961.

Loving, Mabel. *Pony Express Rides On.* St. Joseph, Mo.: Robidoux Printing Co., 1961.

Lucia, Ellis. *The Saga of Ben Holladay.* New York: Hastings House, 1961.

Majors, Alexander. *Seventy Years on the Frontier.* Chicago: Rand McNally and Company, 1893.

Mattes, Merrill J. *The Great Platte River Road.* Lincoln, Nebraska; Nebraska Historical Society, 1969.

Meline, James F. *Two Thousand Miles on Horseback.* New York: Hurd and Houghton, 1867.

Moody, Ralph. *Stage Coach West.* New York: Thomas Y. Crowell Co., 1934.

Morgan, Dale L. (ed.) *Diary of James A. Pritchard from Kentucky to California 1849.* Berkeley: University of California Press, 1963.

Morton, J. Sterling and Albert Watkins. *Illustrated History of Nebraska.* Lincoln, Nebraska: Jacob North, 1907.

Olson, James C. *History of Nebraska.* Lincoln: University of Nebraska Press, 1955.

O'Reilly, Harrington. *Fifty Years on the Trail.* London: Chatto and Windus, 1889. Reprinted Norman, Oklahoma: University of Oklahoma Press, 1963.

Ostrander, Major Alson B. *An Army Boy of the '60's.* New York: World Book Company, 1924.

Root, Frank A. and William Elsey Connelley. *The Overland Stage to California.* Topeka: 1901.

Sanford, Mollie Dorsey. *Mollie* (Diary). Lincoln: University Press, 1959.

Walker, Henry Pickering. *The Wagonmasters.* Norman, Oklahoma: University of Oklahoma, 1966.

Ware, Eugene F. *The Indian War of 1864.* Topeka, Kansas: Crane and Company, 1911.

Webb, William Edward. *Buffalo Land.* Philadelphia: Hubbard Brothers, 1873.

Wellman, Paul I. *Death on Horseback.* Philadelphia: Lippincott, 1947.

Winter, Oscar Osburn. *Via Western Express and Stage Coach.* Leland Standford University, 1945; Reprinted, Lincoln: University of Nebraska Press, 1968.

Writers Program W.P.A. *Sious Lookout Country.* Lincoln: 1942 (Typewritten)

Young, Charles E. *Dangers of the Trail in 1865.* Geneva, New York: Press of W. F. Humphrey, 1912.

Young, Frank C. *Across the Plains in '65.* Denver, 1905.

NEWSPAPERS

Nebraska City News (1857-1867)

People's Press, Nebraska City, Nebraska (1859-64). Some issues missing.

Omaha Daily Republican. September 1, 1865, Francis Lohnas; July 8, 1876, John Andrew Morrow.

Omaha Daily Bee. July 7, 1876, J. A. Morrow.

Stockton California Record. (Reprint Nebraska City News 1923), William Campbell.

Curtis (Nebraska) Enterprise, 1936 Cliffords.

Gothenburg, Nebraska Times, July 27, 1932. George Gilman's letter.

THESES (University of Nebraska)

Bresee, Floyd Edgar. *Oregon Trail 1850-1870.* 1937.

Kiffen, Elizabeth Ardis. *Overland Emigration Through Nebraska 1840-1870.*

Krouch, Mildred. *Geography of the Oregon Trail in Nebraska.* 1933.

Long, Margaret. *Oregon Trail.* 1954.

MISCELLANEOUS

Wyoming Historical Society
    1897 pp. 276-278 Whitehead, Charles. News article from San Francisco Chronicle, June 19, 1881 (Creighton's telegraph and the Indians)

Annals of Wyoming
    XXI: p. 211 Description of Sherman
    XVII: p. 1-56 Stockmen
    XXXIX: #2, pp. 187-216. Clough, Wilson O. Mini-aku

Kansas Historical Society
    Quarterly: XIII: p. 498 Leavensworth Pike's Peak Co. Weather 1859-69

Nebraska Historical Society
    Vol. IV: p. 115 Campbell, William—Letter
    VI p. 82 Fitchie, S. D.—Article
    XXVIII pp. 176; 239-260 Haggerty, J. C.
        "Indian Raids Along the Platte and Little Blue Rivers 1864-65."
    XV: p. 92 Pattison, J. J. Diary

Road Ranches on the Oregon Trail
    XVI: p. 121
    XXIX: p. 190 Thomas Alfred Creigh. "From Nebraska City to Montana 1866."
    V: p. 48 James Green. "Plum Creek Massacre"

National Archives
    39th Congress House of Representatives
    2nd Session (Ex. Doc. #23)

46th Congress Senate Misc. Doc. #19 Holladay's itemized losses

Sitgreaves papers

Records of United States Army Command (Army Posts) 34 items concerning contracts between Gilmans and the Quartermaster Corps.

Fort McPherson Records

Copies of telegrams sent from post 1863-67

Records 1865-67

Majors, T. J. Personal Papers: Folder V Military Documents, Oct. 1863—April 6, 1876. N.S.H.S.

North, Joshua N. 2 personal letters 1862. 1864 N.S.H.S.

Phillips, P. C. (Ed.) Upham Letters from Upper Missouri 1865

Rules and Regulations for the Government of Russell, Majors, and Waddell Outfit. Nebraska City: Thomas Morton ca 1859

Post Returns Gilman Station 1964-1965

Suttie, Mrs. James. *Pride of My Hands* (pamphlet) Omaha: 1962

The Trail, #7 pp. 7-15 "D. C. Oakes, the Man who Wrote the Guide Book."

Harpers Magazine, 1867: "A Stage Ride to Colorado."

Territorial Census 1860

Territory of Nebraska: Lincoln County Record Books I and II

McDonald, Charles, Cash Books of the McDonald Road Ranch at Cottonwood Springs, 1864-1867 (A portion missing) N.S.H.S.

Paine, Bayard H., *Pioneers, Indians and Buffaloes.* (Pamphlet) Curtis, Nebraska: Curtise Interprise, 1935.

Courtney, W. B., *Pony Boy.* Collier's Magazine, August 9, 1930.

MAPS

Harvey, August F. (Civil Engineer). *Routes to the Gold Region, Colorado Territory,* 1862.

Department of the Interior. *Map of the Western Division of the Fort Kearney, South Pass and Honey Lake Road,* 1857.

Bureau of the Corps of Engineers, *United States and their territories between the Mississippi River and Pacific Ocean,* 1850.

Surveyor General Office (Plattsmouth, Nebraska), *Original surveys of the southeastern portion of Lincoln County Townships 11 and 12 North, Ranges 26-28 West,* 1869.

University of Nebraska, *State Soil Survey, Department of Conservation and Survey Division,* G. E. Condra, Dean and Director, 1923.

Counties: Perkins, Keith, Lincoln, Dawson, Buffalo, Kearney, Phelps, Gosper

INDEX

219

220

221

222